Bonding

A Somatic-Emotional Approach to Transference

Stanley Keleman

edited by Gene Hendrix

Center Press, Berkeley

Published by Center Press
2045 Francisco Street
Berkeley, California 94709

ISBN 0-934320-11-X

Designed by Randall Goodall

Table of Contents

Introduction

From a somatic perspective transference and counter-transference are more than emotional and psychological phenomena. They are, most importantly, how a person forms himself and gives meaning to his experiences by how he bonds to and separates from others. How a person bonds to another involves processes and action patterns which are cellular, motoric, muscular attitudes.

Transference and countertransference refer to how a client and a therapist develop a relationship with each other to individuate, seek satisfaction, or maintain their social, instinctual, and personal lives. The past experience of each, concretized in their ongoing bodily structure and process, shapes their present bonding.

A client comes with physical complaints, sexual difficulties, authority issues, lack of self-esteem or interpersonal concerns, but whatever his presenting problems, somatic bonding is a significant element in what takes place between a helper and the person seeking help. Verbal interaction is a part of this process but so are the somatic-muscular stances that the therapist and client assume. This is true irrespective of the particular school of therapy that the therapist offers. For example, the helper may project an attitudinal stance of being big and mothering while the client invokes the stance of being small and helpless. As the therapy progresses, the client may become more helpless and small or, if the helper does not look or act big or accepting, the client responds with muscular attitudes — cautious restrained breathing, stiffened fingers or toes, tightened abdomen and anus. The therapist feels increasing demands and makes his own response. He stiffens his neck or mouth in an attitude of rejection, or tries to appear at ease in order to cover his own lack of response to the increased calls for help. The client, in turn, experiences these somatic signals as rejection or disapproval.

Therapeutic relationship, then, is a bond of muscular motoric attitudes and expressions as well as feeling and counterfeeling. Bonding, as used in this monograph, refers to both the client's and the therapist's somatic patterns, what the psychological literature calls transference and countertransference. Transference includes the muscular response patterns by which the client bonds to the therapist. Countertransference also includes the helper's somatic responses — the ways he accepts or rejects the client's somatic, emotional states. This bonding is a continuing process of muscular, attitudinal, emotional postures and involves voluntary as well an involuntary responses. In these lectures, transference and countertransference are viewed as artificial poles of a singular relational continuum and the term bonding is used to refer to this continuum.

It is this aspect of somatic therapy which differentiates it from more traditional approaches which focus solely on feelings, emotions, fantasies, and images. Somatic therapy views bodily gestures and motoric expressions as the real mirror for feelings and needs. The interaction of somatic-emotional postures and gestures between the therapist and the client is what establishes the bond or ongoing system between them.

To identify this system and to be able to disorganize it is the goal of this monograph. It is based on a series of lectures given during 1984-1985 in which somatic transference was viewed as a process of bonding, a progression similar to the developmental patterns from fetal life to adulthood. The lecture format presents the central theme of bonding through a variety of overlapping frameworks which assume practical significance in selected case studies and as the reader engages in self-reflection questions. This format encourages a dialogue between the material presented and the reader's clinical experience.

Lecture One

Transference and countertransference describe very concrete phenomena—the process by which a person tries to form a connection with another person and what dynamics occur as a person connects for whatever reason. There are work connections and love connections, and so forth. For example, some people need to turn everyone into an authority while others turn everyone into subordinates. Each is based on individual needs. A somatic process perspective starts with the kind of bond or connection a person is trying to form with the helper and the kind of responses to bonding that a helper wants to form with him. Transference and countertransference are forms of bonding, forms of connection, ways to create behavior.

Connection and Distance: The Meaning of Bonding

The somatic process model of bonding starts with how the highly animated egg begins to connect in the uterus. A real dialogue begins: "I am part of you, yet I am not a part of you. I need to be part of your for my own well-being and growth, so don't get rid of me even though I seem to be a foreign body. Can you accept who I am even though I am not you?" In human words, these are the basic conversations that occur on the uterine level. Asked differently, how do the immunological systems of the mother and the growing fetus come to some neutralized state in which neither one rejects the other? How does an animate piece of protoplasm connect to another yet retain some separation while it maintains the urge to bond and unite? This question is the key to every stage of relationship.

These basic dynamics—the relationship of the mother to the child and the child to the mother—is the analog for all bonding phenomena. The quality and quantity of distance and connection are established early on. This forms first as a prepersonal relationship, a genetic relationship, a relationship before individual personality as we understand it. Distance and closeness are regulated right at the beginning. There is a venous and arterial blood exchange, a pulsatory phenomenon starting with laking and continuing with the formation of tubes and pulsatory waves. This is the beginning of duality, "I and thou."

This is what goes on, the growing fetal structure wants unlimited responses yet has to wait for the placental pump to deliver. Bonding begins with duality.

With birth comes a second stage, a personal stage, the child-mother relationship. This is like the uterine connection only the whole surface of the mother's body and the breasts now form the connection. There is the possibility for more closeness and distance than what occurred in the womb. Yet there is still the same struggle— "you" and "me," separate yet connected. Later on father and siblings are introduced and there is no longer a dualistic system but a triadic one. So the first two levels involve mother and child, first, prepersonally and then personally, hopefully, in a connection of caring. The introduction of the father as a figure introduces society. It doesn't have to be the father per se, it could be other relatives, but it is the introduction of a societal impulse. These interactions result in the three layers of the self—prepersonal, personal, and post-personal.

The pulsatory continuum of expansion and contraction is related to the forms that are undergoing development. In the womb the pulsatory continuum creates an embryological environment for the child and maternal forms for the mother. Her body changes, she no longer is a woman but is in the process of becoming a mother. The shape of her belly, the shape of her breasts, her hormonal changes, changing fat distribution—all organize the changing of her form as the embryological changes go on. This is an external reflection of the dialogue moving back and forth between the fetus and the mother. Post-uterinely, the pulsatory continuum builds on this first bonding to create a young child and then a maturing child. This again changes the shape of the mother, she gives up lactating and begins a dynamic interaction with the child as a person. A completely different form emerges. Other forms of behavior emerge as she relates to the child swinging between mother and woman and teacher. Then, with the triadic relationship of father and others, sociological imperatives are introduced, the beginning of distance and objectivity. Connection and bonding have to do with how experience gets organized, how it is transferred to others, and how it is introjected to become a part of one's self.

The Purpose of Bonding:
Creating, Maintaining, or Disorganizing Form

Contact, the pattern of closeness and distance, serves a function. That function is mutual interaction to sustain a form or develop an emerging form. A client comes to a helper because he is in a crisis about organizing his life or moving on to the next stage. It is an error to think of therapy as a process of regressing the patient, taking him back to something in order to overcome his deprivation or emotional injury. Somatic process work does not accept this viewpoint. It believes that each person has an inbuilt urge to undergo the stages of transformation from embryo to adult. This investment in the future determines the dynamics of the present relationship. For the growing child, contact is not organized for its immediate pleasure or welfare. It is part of an essential supportive environment that takes the child from embryo to fetus to baby to young child to adolescent. The relationship of the child to its mother or other persons is in the service of these developing forms. So a patient tries to relate in such a way that it permits him to pick up where he is and where he was in order to go forward and make his next shape.

A client projects onto the helper those qualities that he needs for his own growth. Those same qualities will be introjected and become part of his form in the next stage of his development. Projection is a process which expresses the way a person knows how to exist in the present as well as his urge to establish that kind of relationship which will take him the next step. "I need an authoritarian figure to give me boundaries. Those boundaries represent my need to channel myself and focus on what is at hand. These limitations give me self-identity."

A client may be seeking a therapist to establish boundaries for him. He will provoke, test, even give the therapist qualities that he does not have. For example, a client may say, "you are so orderly, Stanley, in how you planned that lecture." But I am an intuitive thinker, not a compulsive planner. This person needs to see me as orderly in order to have a reaction to his own orderliness and deal with it for his own growth. He puts something on me in order to take it back. It is not a projection but how he organizes to deal with his own logic-making function and then takes it back. For a child, all functions are initially perceived as external; it is a developmental step when he internalizes them. As he does so, his individuality grows.

To recap: transference is what a client brings to the therapist as his emotional state, and how he sees the therapist or his world in those moments when he permits himself to peak through his acceptable social facades. "Since I don't have to be rational or polite to you, let me tell you how I see the world or see you." This is transference, the projection forward of a client's emotional environment as it was, as it is, and as he wishes it to be. "You aren't my rejecting father, are you?" a client will ask. But what if he needs a rejecting therapist in order to bond differently? There is nothing wrong with a therapist who uses rejection as long as he knows that he does and forms a truthful bond so that the client learns to deal with this reality.

Bonding: A Somatic Process

William Condon of the University of Pittsburgh studied the roots of language and discovered it was based on the motoric interchange between mother and child. His work indicates that language, the use of the voice, rhythmicity and melodiousness are assymetrical. In other words, the mother's voice, rocking or twisting movements, and the child's natural rocking and twisting movements are part of a communication process. What Condon's work means to a somatic process perspective is that motor behavior is the basis of human mothering and communication. Patterns of muscular-emotional behavior are the substrata of bonding for the mother and child. Patterns of movement expand from basic intrauterine pulsations to hunger and breast feeding to language, all the while developing the skeletal and organ muscle movements of contact and distance.

Seeking closeness and being separate are patterns that extend throughout the whole of life. Life begins with given programs of behavior that seek development and response and the development of human shape calls for ongoing dialogue and interaction. Patterns that are genetically programmed begin the developmental process. These patterns acquire social and personal meaning through association and experience. When a child is not responded to, he cries out for help and wails in anger hoping both to make contact and have some control over the mother or himself. The feeling of helplessness and the need to be protected are images we all recognize. The cramped, shortened, agitated, breath-holding, red-faced spasm of the infant provokes emotional concern. Parents respond to this somatic, emotional, visual image with muscular and visceral actions of concern, investigation, help. Muscular response comes before feeling. A mother responds reflexively, she moves to provide assistance.

This same symphony is repeated during childhood, adolescence, and adulthood. Children cringe, act helpless, become small when they want a different response from their parents, more closeness or more distance. Children learn to alternate acting big and small. A child becomes small when he wants the parent to be big, protective, or take charge. Likewise a child will stiffen up, be big and brave, cease crying, or be strong when he wants to be grown-up or more adult-like.

A person's muscular-emotional patterns acquire given meaning by his unique history. Parents and siblings respond to patterns of acting helpless, seeking intimacy, pushing away, seeking independence or domination. A child internalizes these responses and, in turn, acquires further motoric responses to deal with these patterns. Over time, these responses become habitual.

These patterns are generally unconscious; they happen without his knowledge. Either he rationalizes his actions or he lacks knowledge about what he seeks with his muscular-emotional postures. A person may verbally ask for help yet unconsciously posture himself in a stance of denial or his helplessness may be covered by a stance of pride. Too often, unfortunately, a person pays attention to his internal dialogue only on the mental or emotional levels. He neglects the somatic-motoric aspects and therefore is likely to misunderstand the responses he elicits from others and never resolve his conflicts about closeness and distance.

Bonding: A Cyclical Process of Moving to the World and Back to the Self

Bonding involves a pulsatory wave that goes through cycles of expansion and contraction, closeness and distance. Not all distancing by a patient is hostile. Not all coming forward is aggressive. The pulsatory continuum of projected needs and desires and images of the world is also accompanied by a retreat, a withdrawal, a self-gathering, a resting. The initial projections and introjections in the interview and the following sessions create the bonds that then follow a cyclical pattern. As the therapist moves toward the client and away from him, he moves toward and away from you. He projects, introjects, incorporates, and re-emerges. Part of the countertransference is how you respond to his cyclical behavior. When the client withdraws or is passive, do you say that he is hostile or depressed? If a person has an urge to regulate himself and the emerging forms of his behavior, then there is a clearer image of what his closeness or distance means.

It is important to know how a client bonds. If a client tries to make you a well-ordered logical person and you aren't, you could look for the function of his projection. Is the function to distort reality so he feels safe? It may be a statement about himself projected onto you in order to take it back. If a person sees you as logical, you can talk about how he uses his own logic. He can then take back what is his and you can admit that you aren't very logical.

Bonding has to do with the therapist's ability to understand himself. A therapist may find that a client sees something in him that he doesn't know about himself. Perhaps the client sees the therapist as a cold, rejecting person. If the therapist has a stake in seeing himself as warm and accepting, then he must deny the client's projections. But the client who says that the therapist is cold and distant may be asking him to be that way so the client isn't trapped by guilt or empathy. Perhaps this client had a mother who always wanted him to be warm, and he resented that, so he now makes the therapist cold so as not to be trapped as before.

I am not sure that a client always tries to establish a relationship that is comfortable for him. He may need to organize a situation that is non-threatening but that is something different. I tell my daughters that it is hard to grow up and they agree. It helps them to understand their difficulties in being cooperative, or getting along with each other. But some mothers say "don't be unhappy." What if the child's unhappiness has nothing to do with the mother? It may have to do with the child struggling with his own reality.

The main tools a therapist has are his own responses. To be able to examine his coldness in terms of its function, how he responds to what this person evokes in him and to understand its place in dealing with the client—that is what needs to be addressed. A therapeutic process is not objective. Even if a therapist keeps a distance, it is still a personal relationship. "I keep distant, because I am tempted to be friendly, and I don't want to be," or "I have to be cold because you are a very attractive, or seductive, or manipulative person, and I have to defend myself." Or a therapist might say, "It is useful for you to deal with distance because you are always trying to make the world friendly and get it close to you."

Lecture Two

Bonding: A Normal Phenomenon

An examination of somatic and emotional transference and countertransference reveals that they are like any other phenomena of human behavior—they define a relationship but in a special way. My view is that transference and countertransference are normal phenomena. They occur in every single relationship where one person assumes a position of authority while the other person assumes a position that is not equal—for example, between a parent and a child, a teacher and a student, or a boss and his subordinate. And the reason these are normal phenomena is that they are the mechanisms by which bonds of communication are established.

The attempt to bond establishes pathways, tunnels, channels of communication. In practicing therapy it is important to understand that reliving an emotion or a piece of the past is not the essential mechanism. What primarily happens is the attempt to establish a bond, a pathway of communication in whatever ways the client and therapist can.

Some bonds are meant to test the therapist. "Is this going to be like the past?" "Are you just like my mommy and daddy?" These are the questions. But testing is a secondary mechanism. The primary purpose is to establish a bond or communication pathway between the client and the therapist. When looked upon as an attempt to establish a somatic-emotional bond of communication, transference is put into a different light. For example, I have trouble with my patient, Mary. She comes to my office and in fifteen minutes I am ready to go to sleep. I find she bores me. If I come up with something she tries to dampen it by perpetually complaining or depressiveness. The fact of the matter is that a patient makes a bond with which he feels comfortable and the therapist responds, not in an idealized way, but in a way that makes him the other part of the bond or communication system. In the example given above, the therapist becomes connected by his drowsiness or by his unwillingness to participate emotionally.

Transference, then, is an attempt to establish an emotional or somatic pathway. Put poetically, transference and countertransference is an attempt to establish soul connections, to somatize needs, to make a lived body. Clients come to therapists with a variety of presenting problems, yet want to deal with them through an emotional connection or a bond of intimacy.

How do you as a therapist communicate with your clients? If your communication is, "I don't want you too close," or "I am listening but I am not your mommy," then these stances become the basis of the relationship. The client will persistently try to get you to respond differently. That is why he repeats his behavior, to get a response, any response. Alienation results when he fails to get a response and it is the most viscious of punishments. Our penal system is built on this—it deprives a person of intimate and free contact with others hoping that this will teach him not to repeat his crime. Unfortunately, too often, some therapists do not understand that many cries for help are not that at all, they are cries for contact. These expressions of helplessness are intended to make contact and begin a connection by which the client will grow.

If you work somatically with someone, it is very important to know how you bond somatically and emotionally. You have to know what is happening in you muscularly as well as at the feeling level. Then you can learn to manage your responses. You can begin with the recognition that you are limited situationally by your ability to be responsive. Furthermore, responsiveness is as much a muscular and somatic organization as it is an emotional one.

Therapeutic Vision

It is important to identify your own therapeutic vision if you are to understand the transference situations that come up in your practice. For example, the strategy of frustrating the client, letting impulses be expressed but not gratified, is an attempt to build a transference relationship with a client. It also intensifies the client's instinctual needs so he can look at them and the kinds of associations he has and thus gain self-knowledge. Therefore, frustration or nonresponse by the therapist is an attempt to teach the client to find both what he wants and how he goes about it without having to rely on the therapist.

Countertransference means the responses the therapist has to the client's needs, associations, or attempts to bond. The therapist's own motor and emotional conflicts then become an integral part of the therapy yet may not involve the client. The bonding relationship intensifies the transference and lets the client experience early somatic-emotional states. The therapist's response helps the client look at what has happened and organize a different response.

In the process of therapy, this bonding or relationship undergoes challenge and reformulation. There is no one attitude that continues throughout the entire therapy. If there is, it is artificial. Therapy is a series of changing relationships. At some point either the therapist or the client may not want to go any further, or the therapy bogs down because neither is capable of disorganizing the relationship he has in order to form another bond. Because the therapeutic encounter primarily involves an exchange of feeling, the therapist must know what he can accept and what he can live with, while at the same time not exploit the person who has come for help.

In the process of bonding, an individual attempts to establish, in whatever way possible, a give and take to the relationship in order to maintain normal aliveness. Reaching out is one way to do this, but so is the opposite, distancing. The effect of distancing is for the other to follow which is an attempt to create a bond. Care must be exercised not to analyze this process away or break it down because the client may not know how to establish any other kind of connection, and neither may the therapist.

It is often thought that freeing a client from his projections establishes another kind of connection but experience proves this is often not so. Because of the assumption that the psyche will find a way to reconnect, much misery is created in therapy. In fact, the organism may not have the wherewithal to construct, either quickly or if ever, a communication bond other than the one in existence. Somatic-emotional therapy does not disorganize behavior until it provides a matrix that encourages the other to form himself.

Pulsation: The Basis of Bonding

Pulsation is the basic reality of animate existence, an event that continues over time as an undulating peristaltic wave. Pulsation involves a continuous circulation and the fate of this circulation is what bonding is all about.

Pulsation is an organismic event. The entire soma pulsates in a resonating wave that changes shape. This shape-changing evokes quantities and qualities of feeling and is linked to how a person functions. We expand with desire and appetite, we come back to ourself when satiated or satisfied.

A person's changing shape reveals his energy, feeling, and how he functions. Imagine a child sucking at his mother's breast and the different kinds of sucking engaged in—vigorous aggressive actions connected to hunger and the softer soothing actions similar to umbilical peacefulness. The mother responds with a variety of shapes—softness, contact, giving, indifference, resistance, rigidity. So the shapes an organism experiences during its intensification of pulsation with others are important. Some of these shapes are genetically given, for example, getting, taking, reaching, receiving, giving, expecting, needing, rage and crying. When the shape of a person's need is interfered with, his function and expression become distorted: biting replaces sucking, he shrinks or he feeds in such a way that he resists swelling with hunger and assertion.

Life begins with a uterine bond, an embeddedness that establishes a close pulsation and conveys acceptance and connection. A deep feeling of tidal oneness evokes the shape of the embryo, fetus pulsating from the navel. Oxygen, food intake, excretion all take place in an unbroken chain of pulses, expand, pause, shrink, push, pause, receive, penetrate, pause, be penetrated. All this time the closed space of the womb and the entire outer surface of the membranes of the intrauterine fetus pulsate. This union of expansion and contraction establishes the cellular shapes of connection, acceptance, warmth, and growth.

At birth, this state of continuous pulsation shifts. The unbroken connection of abdomen-navel is interrupted. Pulsation shifts to the upper body when breathing takes place through the nose and nutrition takes place through the mouth. The pulsatory waves previously located in the arterial tree give way to respiratory pulsation in the lungs and upper digestive tube. Air, food, and body warmth are now sought through connections that are episodic. As pulsations intensify we reach out strongly to restore the bond that means food and closeness. The need for a response is imperative. As this occurs repeatedly, we develop a sense of self-mastery; the world is there and can be called upon to respond. If, however, we receive little response, delayed response, or lack of response, anger, fear, helplessness, or dread are invoked. Upper body development linked with the connection that makes us integrated is the foundation for creeping, crawling, walking, the use of the voice and gesture—our links to action.

Birth changes the nature of bonding. At birth we bond skin to skin, nervous system to nervous system, but the previous fetal connection can be reconstituted on demand. As this mouth-breast stage deepens, we learn about connection, a sense of belonging, the nature of response, and the beginning of self-control and the control of others. As the ability to control our connections to others increases, we form different relationships with the sources of our comfort, security, and emotional environment as well as to our own needs. When another is no longer there on demand, we learn to control our urges and develop the need for feeling contact rather than simple instinctual connection.

With the maturation of genital organs, pulsation again shifts from the upper body—mouth, chest, head—to the lower body—abdomen, pelvis, genitals. When pulsation intensifies the feelings in these areas our self image and functioning change. With the impulse to bond genitally comes an urge to establish different connections with another. In the genital phase contact is again episodic so, once again, we must learn to sustain contact and regulate our needs. With the next great evolution of pulsation, the body-to-body phase, we have the chance to complete the bond of pulsatory circulation, to be in one's self and yet sustain that with another. When instinct is not the driving force, we can learn to sustain the contact and complete the circulation of pulsation within ourselves whereas before we had to learn to control incomplete connections and broken contact.

The four stages of bonding, Chart One, involve a shifting location of the pulsatory continuum linked to differentiated learnings about connection, contact, and control. We move from 1) a continuous unbroken fusion of self and other, to 2) an episodic demand-driven upper body connection, to 3) an intense lower body connection, to 4) the sustaining of continuous pulsation internally and externally. Connection begins with fusion, union, embeddedness, where we are the other more than ourselves. Then connection changes to an episodic demand, a separate longing for the other whom we now identify with. Then connection becomes a demand that seeks recognition from the other, we identify with our need and demand the other do so also. Finally, connection becomes identifying with ourself as well as another in separate and joint interactions. Contact shifts from 1) a given, to 2) a demand, to 3) a controlled need, to 4) an internalized experience, and control changes from external to internal to a combination of the two.

To the therapist it is significant how a client has passed through these stages and how he tries to connect, control, or make contact in his way. A client may become stuck in a particular type of bond that he cannot separate from, or try to re-establish one that was incomplete for him. It is important how a client attempts to bond with the therapist and how he uses himself to form shapes of connection, contact, and control. Is the client a dependent child, passive or aggressive? Is he too demanding? Does he control or resist control around taking, getting, giving? Does he resist receiving another? Does he suck in, pull back, assume the shape of a concave taut shell? Does he feel so entitled to that he swells with aggression, taking stances of attack and penetration? Does he pull back or push forward?

Transference has to do with re-experiencing one's urge for connection, for control, and for contact and forming new ways to bring it about. It is about trying to get control of one's needs for connection, to feel in control or not in someone else's control, to create contact with another rather than always wait for contact or avoid it because it means loss of control.

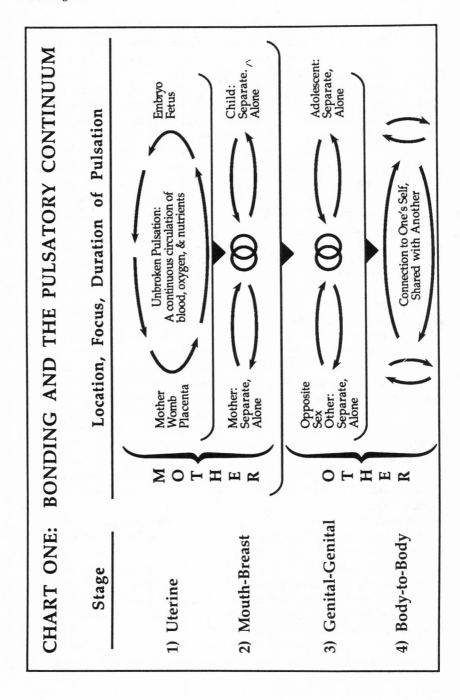

CHART ONE: BONDING AND THE PULSATORY CONTINUUM

Location, Focus, Duration of Pulsation

Stage

1) Uterine

M
O
T
H
Mother
Womb
Placenta

Unbroken Pulsation:
A continuous circulation of
blood, oxygen, & nutrients

Embryo
Fetus

2) Mouth-Breast

E
R
Mother:
Separate,
Alone

Child:
Separate,
Alone

3) Genital-Genital

O
T
H
Opposite
Sex
Other:
Separate,
Alone

Adolescent:
Separate,
Alone

4) Body-to-Body

E
R

Connection to One's Self,
Shared with Another

When his attempts to bond are interrupted, a person becomes angry, fearful, hyperactive, helpless, submissive, depressed, or defeated. If this blocked connection happens intrauterinely, spontaneous abortion results. If it occurs mouth-to-nipple, an inflated inflamed chest of anger and fear is created. The child fears abandonment or lack of response and feels helpless to control his own needs or others. A sense of unworthiness may arise.

At the genital level a person may lack contact with others or fear always having to control himself. He ends up afraid of rejection and his self-confidence diminishes. Or he becomes angry and rageful to make the other submit to him. Alternately, he becomes apathetic and resigned if controlled by the other.

A lack of connection, control, and contact destroys individuation and separateness, and makes one overvalue or diminish others. Either we keep away from others altogether or never get away from them. We become outraged, fearful, submissive, or defeated. Accompanying these states are projections that seek to perpetuate a bond or try to overcome it. The therapist becomes who a client needs for the client's projections to continue. For example, a client who has difficulties in reaching out projects onto his therapist the rationalization for his own inner state, "you are withdrawing," "you are rejecting me." This client seeks a therapist who can help him recognize his own stance towards contact and practice reaching out.

The goal in somatic-emotional therapy is to re-establish the pulsatory continuum. Therefore the therapist is asked to take on roles that complement the four stages of bonding—as womb, as provider of nourishment, as resonator/acceptor of sexual pulsations, as adult guide and friend. A therapist should not fall into the trap of establishing the "hurtful parent" response, neither should he become the "good parent." Rather the therapist is the other whose response can help the client form his pulsations into the differentiated levels of human interaction. Transference is the process whereby the client creates his view of the therapist as he needs him to be—a receptacle for himself, a way to organize his behavior. A therapist's responses make him either part of a predetermined system or a system undergoing formation. The great potential of transference is the possibility for the client to learn anew to love and be loved, to make contact and connection while maintaining control of himself.

Four Levels of Bonding

The pulsatory continuum creates these four levels of bonding: the fetus-uterus-placenta, the mouth-breast, the genital, and the body-to-body level of generalized social contact. The developmental level by which the client functions determines the nature of the transference.

Embryo-Uterus-Placenta. On this level transference is without discrimination. The client needs to be received in either a welcoming or unwelcoming womb. The client invades, pushes in, fuses with the therapist. He has an urge to be implanted and to break down the blood vessel walls in order to make a bond. The goal is to exchange nutrients.

This type of transference involves the psychology of implantation and the transference of energies to support it. Gigantic hormonal and biochemical changes take place in the egg-embryo and in the uterus-mother, all going on under the surface, below the thresholds of knowing, below personality. This type of transference, therefore, has little to do with mutual trust.

The embryo-uterus-placenta level is one of continual activity. There is little silence in the uterine connection. There is a constant exchange of nutritive substances and the beginning of the exchange of social substances. The placenta level grows to the next stage where there is body contact and the beginnings of behavior.

The following illustrates this type of bonding and the counter-transference response of the therapist:

> *Woman therapist:* I have a schizophrenic patient where the bond is good. She called me recently and left a message on my answering machine that said, "Hello, baby, I am cancelling today." She then asked if at the next session I would look with her at her baby pictures. I had an angry response to that. She always intrudes into my life, and I allow her more intrusions than I want. Yet, in the context of these stages maybe she is sending me a different message.
>
> *Stanley Keleman:* She called you "baby?"
>
> *W.T.* She needs control so I interpret her message as, "I will treat you the way I want you to treat me."
>
> *S.K:* I would say she is on the level of intrusion which she can't help. This is the level of implanting, the embryo-uterus-placenta level. There are forces in operation here which are below personality. She is trying to find a womb to lock into, therefore she invades, intrudes. The quality of her insistence provides the clue to the nature of the bond. And you and I could discuss how you resist implantation.

Mouth-Breast. Transference at this level is characterized by its episodic nature. Qualitatively, it contrasts with the embryo-uterus-placenta level since the client is more insistent but less invasive.

After birth there is body contact between mother and child, between the outside of their bodies. This produces contact and stimulates the senses. The nervous system of the child never feels itself unattached. However, this is episodic, governed by the child's hunger or his need for quieting. The ongoing connection of the womb has been replaced by separation and then reunion. The child must find a way to bring the mother to himself. This bonding takes place through the sensory apparatus in contrast with the literal bonding of the embryo-uterus-placenta. Mouth-breast bonding is characterized by a perpetual hunger on the part of the client, a demand for immediate gratification, and a need to be taken care of.

Sexual-Genital. This type of bonding is characterized by the bringing together of gender opposites while maintaining a connection to the similar sex. One is impelled to move from a position of separation to one of connection. This involves approaching the other or attracting the other. In the genital stage the intimacy of early nurturance or its lack is transferred to another. A client looks to the therapist to have his gender affirmed or to establish adult sexuality. The goal is the same feeling state as in the umbilical state, but with the connection occuring through the genitals.

In this type, transference can be troublesome. While a therapist can connect emotionally and encourage somatic gestures on all the other levels, how is he going to make a connection or bonding on the sexual-genital level and not violate the rules of the client and society? A lot of problems arise when a client or therapist likes titillation or stimulation or needs some kind of non-genital but gender excitation to enhance their feeling of masculinity or femininity. It is similar to racing your engine while keeping the brake on or forming a secretive sexual-platonic bond which eventually breaks out in anger and mutual accusations since neither side is able to act on the feelings and sensations that are there.

At this level there is bound to be seductive behavior. The client ceases to be totally a client because his own gender role-playing needs to be enhanced. He wants a union to give him solidity in the world. One way to deal with this situation is to discuss it openly. Other choices are either to end the therapy, keeping in mind that every bond has an implied behavioral aspect, or to deepen the client's sexual involvement with his mate. In any case, it is incumbent upon the therapist to affirm the growing masculinity or femininity of the client.

The following illustrates how one therapist responds to sexual-genital bonding.

> *Male Helper:* I have a woman client who fits this category. I feel she hasn't learned much from her experience in therapy.

My projection is that she sexualizes my touch. And that makes me shy away.

Stanley Keleman: Many people who have had severe contact problems in early life will sexualize their contact later on. How do you touch her?

M.H: I give her a hug after a session.

S.K: Why?

M.H: Sometimes she requests it.

S.K: How do you embrace her?

M.H: I just put my arm around her.

S.K: If a client sexualizes her experience of my embrace, she always can. But in order for her to sexualize the experience, she has to have some bait from the other end. It is a two-way street. So let us discover your side of the problem. Say more about touching.

M.H: A lot of my touch is approach-avoidance. I race the engine with my brakes on. I recognize the stimulation then I retract.

S.K: How old is this woman?

M.H: College age, about twenty-one.

S.K: Does she continue to proposition you?

M.H: She has never propositioned me. In the beginning her presenting problem was marital. She would fantasize and write me letters saying "I would like to meet someone like you."

S.K: How did you handle that?

M.H: We talked about it. I expressed some discomfort with that as we had work to do and I wanted a work relationship.

S.K: How did you think she would respond to your rejection?

M.H: On one level she wanted it, but on another she didn't.

S.K: What did you do with this?

M.H: I never resolved it.

S.K: How come?

M.H: I don't know.

S.K: What is your side of it?

M.H: It was unreal. I bring myself to the therapy but I can't change the type of bonding she wants.

S.K: Are you afraid of her sexual energy?

M.H: If it materialized.

S.K: Why don't we explore that. Are you afraid of her sexual energy?

M.H: Yes.

S.K: How come?

M.H: I would feel exploited. Then I would not be dealing with a therapeutic situation.

S.K: What kind of problems does she have at home?

M.H: No contact with her husband.

S.K: What is your stake in denying the kind of bonding she wants? You are a young man and she is a young woman. Do you feel too vulnerable? Whether you are attracted to her is not the question.

M.H: What is my mistake in this?

S.K: From what I hear you say, your mistake is this. This woman has marital problems. She sexualizes experience. You reject the projected sexual connection. You insist on another kind of bonding, "not this way, that way." That is what she has struggled with all her life. Because she sexualizes the connection, you may be assuming she wants to go to bed with you. You have to let that fantasy come out. Then you can deal with the nature of the fantasy. What does she want in the fantasy? What does she want to come back? What can't you give her back? What is the emotional intensity? How do you know she wants a romantic involvement? Your own assumptions and frailties set up more complications. What does it bring up in you when she acts this way?

M.H: A part feels it is not right. I am goal-directed. The client comes to me to make a better connection in her life, to feel herself more yet she wants to connect with me.

S.K: Or have sexual feelings with you so that she can get accustomed to them and then transfer them to someone in the outside world. You could take that position. You could say,

"When you are in here you can feel what you want. It is perfectly alright."

M.H: I do that intellectually but on the physical level there is an attraction and I am denying her experience somatically.

S.K: Did you discuss that with her?

M.H: No, but I would like to own up to my experience of her, of rejecting her.

S.K: How would you do this, like you are doing it now?

M.H: Yes.

S.K: Why would you do it that way?

M.H: To let her tune in to where I am.

S.K: That is inflammatory. You would invite her into your own reluctance. You could ask, "How do you feel about me rejecting you?" or "What effect does it have when I deny you access to my other self?" Why not give her a chance to discuss the meaning of her feelings rather than turn those feelings aside? Then you could maintain a bond of warm distance rather than cold distance. You could arrive at a different type of bond from your side. Give her a chance to deflect her romantic images, that is, what is different here than at home, or who you really are rather than her image of you. If she lived with you for ten minutes, she probably would hate you. She has to deflect her idealization.

Body-to-Body. This type of transference involves a bond around activity, tasks, problems rather than instinctual gratification. This level involves emotional cooperation and interdependence, a type of contact which involves the entire body. The basic bond is brain-muscle differentiation whereby the entire organism seeks connection based on mastery of activity rather than instinctual gratification. The client is seeking to change his form, shape his relationships, or master a task of self-transformation. The client is more adult-centered, thus the transference focuses on issues of authority, assertion, self-control. This level is characterized by the client's ability to be separate from the therapist, to be an individual, and form a bond not based on past need or experience but on looking at a problem together.

The previous levels of transference involved situations that were based on an urgent need to live inside the other, feed off the other, or to make contact sexual. The therapist took the role of the adult while the client took a more childlike role. At the body-to-body level the client is grounded in himself in a way that is more self-sustaining, thus self-differentiation with the therapist is maintained. Separation is not aloneness, contact is not fusion. A multiplicity of contact is established in which both the brain and the heart influence the level of contact and distance. Transference is based on the communication of feelings, ideas, and actions to serve the growth of the client. As the client grows so too does the therapist as his knowledge and feelings are challenged. Body-to-body transference enables the client to deepen his maturity and form new responses. It is a mixture of separation and closeness, contact and control, all in pursuit of organizing a personal life.

For example, I had a patient who was studying to be a therapist. Her orientation was psychoanalytic rather than somatic. Much of our work together consisted of her challenging my views and being able to hold her own ground. She wanted her own authority recognized even as she challenged mine. My goal was not to change her orientation but to allow her the space and response to work on her own issues of assertion.

The four levels of transference are based upon different stages of growth and somatic development. Each stage can create problems in connecting a person to himself or others, controlling or resisting other's control, and making contact without having to perform or pretend. The therapist's somatic reaction to each of these stages in the client is what is important. A client's brain can be flooded with pelvic sensations which, in turn, frighten or fascinate him. How does the therapist respond to the sexual level of transference? A client can be frightened or seduced by the pulsations in his mouth and throat. These pulsations invoke deep longing and demands on others or feelings of anger and depression. What is produced in the therapist as he meets the mouth-breast transference level? The rise of pulsations in the abdomen are associated with the need to pull others in or get into others and feelings of incorporation or oblivion. What stance does the therapist take to uterine-placental bonding? The client may have feelings of being too close or too distant, confused about being the same as or different from the therapist. What does the body-to-body level invoke in the helper?

The four stages are based upon a two-fold interactive process: first, how the client responds to the feelings and location of his own tissue aliveness, and second, how he needs another to contain, liven, deaden or express these feelings. The therapeutic task is to help a client form a container or avenue of expression, deprogram past responses, and form pulsatory excitation on the next level.

Bonding and Reorganization

Therapy involves a person who is reorganizing his way of being in the world and his experiences. It is necessary to appreciate how an organism is capable and willing to let go of what is no longer useful for it and reorganize itself in a way which enhances itself. Part of this process is up to the therapist. He must reintroduce stimuli without inflaming. There is a somatic way to do this provided the therapist understands the four levels of bonding. Each level is preceded by an exchange of feelers to see if bonding is possible. A different type of transference and countertransference results.

Reorganization can be likened to the steps of pregnancy. There is an implantation with two solids meeting, the egg and the wall of the uterus. There the two solids set up a network of communication. This is followed by fragmentation as the egg divides and subdivides to create more surface area. Structure breaks down but it is not destroyed, it reorganizes into something new. This breaking apart of the solid and the creation of more surface area is not a collapse. It is the opening of boundaries so that there can be circulation and more feeling. Then there is another reforming. At this stage if the client does not find other ways to express himself, he will have to go back to his old ways of organization. This is what the literature refers to as "being stuck" or fixated.

Some therapeutic circles harbor the illusion that the organism knows what is best for it. But that is often not true. An organism only knows what is best for it in a field of responsiveness. It may know that its environment is unhealthy and that it has to get out, but it only knows this because of the bond it has made. The human being cannot live in isolation. It is wrong to say that the human being never discovers who he is during long periods of alienation. He discovers who he is in response to that alienation.

If an organism does not always know what is best for it, does a client have to be guided? I do not know how a therapist can take responsibility for where a client needs to be guided. What really takes place is simply an exploration of the possibilities of behavior without taking the client by the hand and showing him how. For example, I had a male client with an impotency problem. He could achieve an erection but not maintain it. In the course of our conversation he described his upbringing to me. It was the most emotionally devastating climate you could imagine. As a possibility for him to explore, I suggested, when you enter a woman, one way to get pleasure is to gently move. He looked at me and said, "Nobody every told me that." I suggested he try it. Next session he said, "I had no trouble." That is what I mean by raising possibilities for the client to practice.

Bonding stages occur irrespective of the gender of the therapist or client. A embryo-uterus bond can take place between a male client and a male therapist; a female client can establish a mouth-breast connection with a male therapist. For some clients early intimacy and care was provided by the father while others experienced their mother as the dominant authority figure in the family and the one who provided the reality orientation to the world. One client will say, "I have been rejected so badly by my mother that I can only accept maternal feelings from a man." Another says "My father rejected me so much that I can only accept maternal men." Another exclaims, "I need a forceful male or female to bond to because my father or mother was so weak." Therefore, a client may not need an interaction with a particular gender to go through the various bonds. What is significant is the bond he attempts to establish, the gender of the therapist he chooses to establish it with, and what this means for him.

As therapists we have to ask ourselves both who we are and what contract we have with a particular patient. As therapists, we have an idea of who we are, and who we must be. But do we check this out? We may fail to ask, who do I have to be in this particular interaction. As we pass through particular interactions we have to consider when and how the therapy will end. At some point we may have to change how we are going to relate to the other. We set forth different ground rules, "I am not going to relate to you as the breast any more," or whatever. We establish different conditions, "Now I am going to relate to you on the body-to-body level," for example. So again, you are investigating possibilities of behavior.

Once it is established what kind of bonding and communication exchange a client wants, the therapy is enhanced. But there is another level. What does the therapist want or need from the client? What kind of bond is being called for?

How many of us have heard a patient ask, "What is it I give you?" or "What do you get from me?" or "Why do you put up with me?" Sooner or later every client asks these questions. What he is asking is, "Is there something other than money that is exchanged between us?" Your response reveals something to the patient about himself— his sense of humor, his warmth, whatever he has other than money.

A lot of the provocation that comes from a client is an attempt to penetrate what he thinks we are hiding from him. Are we really understanding? Are we really never going to lose our tempers? Are we really going to be there for him? What is it we really think of him? These are all attempts to establish a channel of communication, a bond.

So a therapist must understand the nature of his bonding and how he facilitates the bonding process or how he thwarts it. It is important to recognize that a client is attempting to make or alter a connection or bond and that you, the therapist, also determine the nature of this connection.

Suzie: A Case Study of
Wanting and Wanting to be Wanted

Suzie came to me complaining she could not have an orgasm or surrender to her husband. There was an air of excitement about her. She was moderately good-looking in a young girl way. Her dress was provocative and attention-seeking, matching her self-image of attractiveness and desirability.

When I interviewed her, I discovered her body was shaped somewhat like a weightlifter's, all shoulders and chest with a narrow pelvis. Her form was like the letter V—small waist, raised chest, broad shoulders, stiffened neck—different from an hourglass female form.

Her excitation had a globality that encompassed everything. I felt flooded by her excitement, as if all my senses were being stimulated by a fine feather. It was a total use of herself—the use of her eyes, her gestures, her choice of words. I recognized that her excitement was really fear, a fear crying out for help. It was the appeal of a female in distress. Once I responded to these cries, once I was taken in, the demands came.

I soon realized that her dense, compacted structure was a heavy plate meant to preserve some form of boundary. She was an un-bounded structure, a pretty girl with a come-hither look. To be taken in, however, was to enter a void. Her global surface excitement aroused the other to become her filler. When I held back and did not respond to her helplessness or invitation, raw fear and desperate clinging emerged. "Don't reject me, I depend on you, I need you," was her cry. Her attempts to incorporate the other into herself turned into clinging, complaints of fear and abandonment, and terror around being separated.

As an unbounded structure, Suzie lived in other people. She picked certain key people to be her womb. She used the tools of seduction and helplessness to attain this goal. She began to project onto me that I was her savior. I was the only one who understood everything she did. She trusted me without reservation yet tested me at every step. I became an integral part of a complicated fantasy, I was the soul to which she could finally be united.

Suzie is an example of uterine-placental bonding. It was as if she was born too early. She was flooded with images of a good mommy, a connection where she would not have to perform, fear rejection, or be abandoned. She stiffened all the muscles of her upper body to stifle her digestive tubes and her accompanying feelings of hunger and longing. When I requested that she undo the contractions in her torso and jaw and give up her Barbie-doll look, anxiety and feelings of emptiness flooded her. She attempted to make me her inside through flattery, coyness, seduction, and compliance. As we worked together and her iron corset softened, she was able to feel her insides and became more willing not to clutch herself. She began to sense an inner identity. When I went on vacation, she became depressed and developed a minor illness but was able to manage since she was feeling something inside her.

The next step was to disorganize her clinging. Severing the clinging stance brought on depression, fear, and eruption. When we began to soften the density of her depressive stance, she was flooded with global anxiety. She became a lonely, lost child without an orientation. She remembered how her mother had left her alone in her room on many occasions or left her alone in nursery schools. Her mother had to work and her father was absent. She began to sense for the first time her state of being unwanted. At ten she was sent to an all-girl boarding school. There her loneliness became unbearable. By squeezing herself she contained her fear and lack of parental connection and began to imitate others in order to appear grown-up.

As we were able to differentiate the child hidden under her adult role, she grasped the reality of being separate without accompanying panic. She could feel a need for contact and ask for it without fear of rejection or panic about exposing her infant to the adult world. For the first time she took a job and began to experience others as both competent and incompetent. As her experience grew she became more critical of me. The savior bubble developed a hole. At this point she began to permit powerful pulsations to descend from her upper body into her pelvis and legs. She would then experience waves of hunger and warmth enlivening her pelvis and these melting sensations gave birth to a womanly feeling. She began to sense the difference between the image of being a woman and the feelings of womanhood.

She became more seductive but told me to keep a distance. She wanted to test what another felt like without cloying or manipulating herself to perform. Her sexual fantasies now gave way to sexual feelings. She found herself no longer willing to be submissive or let another enter her in order to feel her insides. She did not feel obsessed with alleviating her feelings of emptiness or densely holding herself against rejection.

As we organized her state of accepting separation without panic or hysteria, she began to form an active life. Instead of acting as an orphaned waif seeking salvation, she became a young lady growing up, able to be alone. She did not have to war with other women whom she previously viewed either as mothers or rivals. She wanted attention and companionship and took on lovers. But in so doing she became submissive to their wishes and, once again, found herself in abusive relationships much the same as she had been with her husband. She began to avoid male sexual closeness as well as female companionship.

In establishing a bond with Suzie, I had to destructure her projection of me as her savior and loving mother in order to allow her adolescence to emerge. It would have been an error not to permit the uterine-placental and mouth-breast stages to form just as it would have been an error not to unform them once their usefulness had been served. Helping her required the forming of these early bonds to give natural boundaries without demanding that she be a premature adult. She was able to pass through the first three stages of bonding and form a membrane that acted as a barrier to the unanchored images and impulses of her early life. Her personal self was no longer washed away by unchanneled excitation and terror. Our connection allowed her child-like projections to emerge and created the early bonds upon which a more mature bond could be built. In this way she was able to form an adult person.

Once she realized the signals which began to disorganize her, she could bear aloneness. She had formed an inside. She had begun to work cooperatively with others. She no longer had to be a doll to get admiration from others.

Suzie's case demonstrates that a self-image is a somatic organization. The image she had of herself as the desirable doll and her helplessness were organized as dense contractions in her upper torso. When these deep muscular contractions around her digestive tube were disorganized, her uncontained state surfaced. When we reached the fourth level of transference, body-to-body, she was able to sense her boundaries and recognize that someone was there for her. She was then able to create a form for herself. She went from being overbound to being unformed and underformed and then created boundaries for herself and an inside. She reformed herself, literally changing from a weightlifter's wedge shaped body, pulled up, pulled in, a state of terror, to a pear-shaped woman with rounded pelvis and abdomen. She began to get closer to others without clinging or becoming a slave.

For a therapist to feel useful, it is important that he be able to respond to the client's needs. At the same time, it is a trap to become the client's savior. Suzie's rigidity was a mask which covered her infant state. Her messages of provocation and promise could easily be confused with adult sexual stances. Her seductive behavior, the stiff way she used herself, her restrained head movement, her coy look, the lifting of her chest to emphasize her breasts, all served to deaden her pelvic region. She portrayed herself as sophisticated yet underneath she wanted to be wanted. Undoing her social pose brought on a mixture of panic and terror and a collapsed posture. This collapsed state was a statement of "want me," "help me." It was not a sexual statement but a need for another's body to give her an inside. Her early rejection had left her without the introjections a girl receives from her mother, something Suzie still needed.

To be there for the client it is not necessary to respond to his social pose or what his need evokes in you. By sorting out my own emotional and somatic responses, I was not pulled into Suzie's unboundedness to act as her savior. She evoked feeling responses in me of concern and wanting to be of help. I was able to dismantle these responses. Each time I pointed out her emotional message, how much she wanted to be a child who belonged to somebody, and told her that she could not belong to me, she fell into despair, fear, and her unbounded feeling of not having another to mother her. Yet this was the precise point at which I could permit our bond to grow. I could be somebody for Suzie to form a bond with in order to feel herself and grow to the next state. I would not be fused with her but a membrane that allowed her to grow while maintaining a separation. This is how bonds are formed and reformed. I accepted her unbounded state as something she needed temporarily without my becoming the person she needed to permanently bond to. This allowed the next bond to form, one in which separations were not devastating. I held myself out in a person-to-person bond as a promise so that she could fill herself and form a container to live with her feelings without losing herself. She was no longer empty and childlike with only immature desires and impulses that needed adult guidance, but a growing person who could form adult relationships with others.

Her projections were wanting me to want her, a uterine state; being the object of her wanting, a mouth-breast state; and fusing with me, a sexual state. Together these projections indicated she was not in contact with her demanding side. This demanding was childlike, obsessive and oppressive and called forth my anger. When I pointed this out to her, she projected abandonment and panic, behavior meant to blackmail. A central goal of the therapy was pointing out her demanding nature and helping her learn how to handle demands.

I had to understand not only the feelings behind her demands but their connection to her body postures, inflation and upper body rigidity accompanying a confused, weak structure underneath. Her basic attitude was to become the center of attention, a posture of give me, notice me, want me, I want you. Suzie's projection of wanting was, in fact, on the deepest level a wanting to be incubated. As we worked somatically applying the HOW exercise to the pulsations of the four levels of bonding, a fuller pulsating current was established. She was able to create an adult emotional form for herself.

Roger:
A Case Study of Impulsiveness

A client bonds with his therapist in characteristic ways that seem to be ever present. This consistent pattern identifies the person both to others and himself and establishes his behavior as a movement towards or away from his next stage of development.

Roger presented his problem as being unable to contain his rage. He was always angry. His angry stance of screaming or making fists was a characteristic expression whenever he did not get his way. His expression of intimidation accompanied an intensity of attack whether he was in a discussion with someone or if he approached a woman. I thought others might envy his out-of-control state until I realized that it was an attack meant both to control or dominate others, and to get his way. He was a rigid person who had one way to approach his emotional needs which was to get the other to do his bidding. He acted this out by assuming postures of defiance and petulance.

I asked him to tell me how he acted defiant and how he created the role of intimidator. He described blowing himself up, making himself bigger, pulling his chest up, puffing it up, tightening his shoulders, stiffening his jaw. All these movements pulled his excitement into his upper body, made him bigger, and created his menacing look. I pointed out to him that he was, in fact, a screaming child inside an adult's body. I asked him to change shape and disorganize his pulled-up pattern of anger. When he took down the overbounded pattern of attack, he experienced himself as a small child, helpless and scared. We began to realize that his overboundedness was a compensation for his hidden smallness, while his rages were attempts to get what the unbounded child needed but could not get—the attention of and closeness to his parents. When he felt these needs rise in him, he would defend against his feelings by becoming panicked, thrashing about in a state of desperation, and acting out-of-control. This repeated itself. His need for closeness brought forth a response of anger and outrage at being close, humiliated, not understood and then further anger at being dependent while trying to be an adult. He consistently related to others in this adultified child pattern trying to be bigger than he was. His need for closeness would invoke fear, his fear would invoke anger.

We formed a contact whereby he could disorganize or separate from his form as a deprived child, let his child take shape, and find ways to be both small and adult. Throughout this period he projected on me a variety of forms from his past, incompetent father, uncaring mother, demanding authority, and adult friend. I took the role of the adult who could contain his need, affirm his want to be loved, and help him get it from his girlfriend rather than dominate her. My role was to be orderly, fair, and make boundaries. At the same time I could not be overly personal with him, a stance which kept evoking his pattern. His need for acceptance was followed by agitation to make the other understand. I also role-modeled intimidation for him so that he could see his own bully. Gradually our relationship took the form of the interrelationship between a strong animated challenger and an authority figure. This stance formed a cooperative relationship between his child and his adult and he began to accept another's reality as different from his own. He could then form a relationship based on mutual interest rather than his own self-interest.

Roger's life problem involved all four stages of transference described in this paper. At one level he wished to be small again, but this was warded off by his anger. Yet the anger was used to get into the other. At first I thought his anger should be discouraged and contained until I realized that it was a signal to be close. When I destructured my reaction to being invaded, we had long periods of a pulsatory flow between us wherein he felt safe and at peace. Separating from this was hard for him and he responded with attacks of anger until he realized that I was there for him and he could return to that state and be safe. The way for him to return was to disorganize his overbounded chest and shoulders.

At a later point in the therapy he wished simply to receive. He would then leave to try on his own and return to demand that I be there for him. This demand was challenged at one point. Why did he associate taking from me with controlling me? Neither I nor any adult wants to be controlled. He hated it in himself. As I did not respond to his demands, he deprogrammed his overbounded demanding stance. As he did this, he began to feel waves of hunger in his throat and mouth. These scared him. He lived these out by trying to get, get, get, taking everybody in without any accompanying feeling of satisfaction. We worked with this until he could feel needy, take from another, feel satiated, and then wait for his hunger to rise again.

Roger's need to control, dominate, and imprison the other manifested itself on the genital-to-genital level also. He would throw himself into involuntary patterns of sexual abandon with a woman. At the same time he did not want to be under her influence. He would feel humiliated at needing the other and begin to act like a boy imitating a man, demanding that the woman submit to all his demands. He could not tolerate separation. At this level he wanted me to be his guiding father. As I tried to put the responsibility on him, he would again become angry. As this was disorganized, he could see that I was different than his real father. I maintained the dialogue even as I demanded that he stand on his own two feet and manage his sensations and feelings around sexuality.

It was important for Roger to try to form a way to be in the world, first with me, then with others on the job and at home. He had to learn to use himself bodily to form a container for his expression and a channel for satisfaction. To do this he had to let his anger turn to need and not feel resentment or cheated out of his childhood.

The insults Roger experienced resulted in his rooting himself in others. He feared the helplessness and rejection of his internalized parents and thus inflamed himself. His pulsatory state gave rise to needy feelings which scared him. As he accepted his bodily-emotional states, his sense of personhood and maleness developed. His compensatory phallic activity in the service of his childhood need decreased. His stance of intimidation and acting bigger than he was, trying to force closeness, and getting the other to respond to his needs or act as a self-regulator diminished. He repeated with me the only ways he knew how to relate. Yet he envied my power and adultness. Challenging his states enabled him to take charge of his own feelings and pulsations. Instead of responses of anger, rage, and frenzied inflation, he could contain himself within his own body.

As the therapy continued and our relationship changed, we formed a way for him to relate to the four levels of bonding differently. He disorganized his upper inflated, overcompacted chest, head, and neck and organized more form in his pelvis and legs. He formed a somatic self to regulate his own impulses and feelings rather than live impulsively, getting rid of those pulsations that he associated with feeling helpless and needy. His understanding of real manhood increased and his sense of self deepened.

Roger understood his situation and his inflammatory response to all situations enacted as roles of big boy, bully, *enfant terrible*, invasive, raging bull—the consistent factors of his self-image. He experienced how he inflated himself, organized himself muscularly away from his own pulsations and impulses and created an overactive response to project his feelings outward. As Roger dismantled the blownup quality of his structure, he learned how his unformed smallness had been thwarted in its growth and how he compensated for it by acting big. The generation and assimilation of these early pulsations in the pelvis, head, and legs allowed Roger to create new insights and form a less helpless self. As Roger lived with and shaped his feelings, he practiced being in the world as a separate individual, someone who was able to be close without being invasive. He began to relate to another as a separate person rather than as a responder to his needs.

Roger's case demonstrates the transference and countertransference involved as a person changes his overbounded states and reforms himself. I had to contain Roger and not be invaded by his energy and tactics. I also had to teach him the feeling of boundedness by acting as his outer container. Had I maintained my own need not to be invaded, he would have experienced only repression and rejection. By creating a variety of responses to his states, I was able to establish a pulsatory communication that addressed all four levels of his problem and helped form a relationship with him of person-to-person. Forming this relationship required that he set up forms of behavior to deal with his past loss of direction and his need to act bigger than he was. His cellular states as well as his feeling and thinking had to be disorganized and reorganized. Throughout this journey I was alternately uterus, mother, father, older brother as well as an adult friend. He went from knowing his way of acting, to learning the organization of that action, to inhibiting the programmed reflexes, to making new meaning and bonding.

Roger bonded to me by attempting to be big in order to avoid his smallness. These were felt body attitudes reflected in the over-bounded, puffed-up attitude in his upper body and his needy, invasive, intrauterine smallness which gave rise to his emotional behavior and self-perception. Our work together involved movement from the outside to the inside to the middle layers, forming a personal layer for self-management. This emotional-somatic transformation involved a journey of disorganizing his attempts to get into the other and organizing a somatic self for him to live in. At the same time as I disorganized his reactive reflex responses to others, I taught him to organize a history of relationship with another. That is the role of transformation, not only to undo the injuries and insults of the past but to form from them the knowledge of how to reorganize into an adult who is closer to the truth of his own process. Roger arrived at a place where he realized his own strong and vital energies and his penetrating, intense, and feelingful qualities. He learned that his invasion and intimidation also resulted from his high energy level and strong body. Learning to form bonds to accept his own powerfulness as well as the limitations of others was part of his growth. Roger discovered the difference between forming an impulse and merely acting it out.

Lecture Three

To review what has been said so far: transference and counter-transference refer to the processes of bonding and unbonding between a therapist and a client. The central issue is how the client is or is not trying to organize a situation for himself by creating the bond he needs or thinks he needs. "In order to grow-up, I need a connection with you in which you are a "good mommy." A client creates behavior by transferring his historical experience onto the present situation. Basically he is trying to make some sort of present connection or to undo one. This concept is a basic dimension of therapy.

Transference means to bring an internal state to the foreground and project it onto the immediate surround. It is a client's internal state that he brings to the therapeutic situation. At the same time, the therapist tries to behave in a self-controlled or self-inhibited way, for example, "I feel needy but I won't project it onto my client but will try to be objective." When the therapist's needs are in the background, he can either be a benign and neutral observer or a participant. Then the helper has less investment in the countertransference aspect except as he wants or does not want to relate to how the client is trying to bond to him. At that point the whole question of how a therapist conducts his therapy comes up. What type of relationships does he want? But the client's internal state is what comes to the foreground as he tries to form the behavior or conditions that would bring him satisfaction or not. Here is where the postpersonal and personal come into play. A client needs to bond in a uterine, maternal, sexual, or adult way. This begins the major operation a client organizes in his interaction. However, it may not appear that way to the helper. The therapist's response has to do with how he relates to a client's child, adolescent, and adult.

In working somatically with people, a basic therapeutic goal is for the client to reorganize his bodily or emotional shape so he can behave differently. Somatic therapy is not primarily concerned with changing a client's mental images. Therefore the nature of the transference is different insofar as strategies are not needed to cook the transference, to heat up the internal conflict, generate dependencies, frustrate the client and permit his projections as happens in the normal analytic mode. These issues comes to the surface the minute a client engages his somatic-emotional configuration—stiff, rigid, dense, swollen. Once the therapist challenges the client's structure and the role he has—the listener, the objectifier, the passive one, the crazy one—whatever role is somatically organized—what lies right behind that are all the emotional fears that created that role. Layer by layer through the mechanism that forms behavior, the symphony of the past and present with all its associations are there. In that respect, all the helper has to do is pay attention and have a model to interpret what appears. The bonding model, as presented in this lecture, is useful because it is a template of possible ways to connect.

An Overview of the Pulsatory Model

The pulsatory continuum has three layers, a prepersonal layer, a societal, more human layer, and a personal layer. This pulsatory phenomenon seeks contact, connection, and continuity which spells control and form. Contact is on the surface, connection is one layer down, continuity is management of the pulsatory process. Together they make a form. Contact waxes and wanes, sometimes it is strong, sometimes it is not so strong. Real learning begins when the contact is weak but the connection is strong. The client wants to go away, but feels himself connected so he can manage his life.

Contact represents a state that is worked at while connection represents a minimum of personal effort, somewhat like a prepersonal state. A child doesn't need contact with its mother, it needs connection. It will settle for connection and give up contact if that is all that is available. For example, schizophrenics want connection, not contact. They can't handle contact. So they tell the therapist that he is getting too close. Some people want connection inside a community but they don't want intense contact or they want to control it. There are people who comes to group therapy for a long time; they never work or talk. They just like the connection with the group but not contact with the group. It is important for the therapist to recognize the difference between connection, a prepersonal bond, and contact, a personal bond, so that his response is appropriate.

There are **four movements** in the pulsatory continuum:

- The movement toward another, self-extension, expansion, projection.

- The movement of self-gathering, taking back, contraction, ingestion.

- The movement of containment, homeostasis, rest.
- The movement of swelling in preparation for action.

Four distortions or exaggerations may accompany these states:

- An increase in aggression, pushing away, hitting.
- Pulling back, withdrawing, letting nothing enter.
- Freezing, giving in, giving up.
- Swelling to encircle or merge with the other.

The first movement narrows a person's boundaries, the second movement requires pulling back to dismantle boundaries, the third movement freezes a person's boundaries and the fourth movement enlarges a person's boundaries. The first exaggeration, pushing-away, can be linked psychologically with paranoia and projection; the second, pulling-back, can be associated psychologically with depression; the third, hibernation or freezing, is linked to obsessiveness and passivity; while the fourth, swelling, can be linked to mania and hysteria.

So the four movements in the pulsatory continuum are coming out, pulling back, assimilation or containment, and swelling. The four distortions include two overbound, pushing away, hitting out, overactivity; pulling away, coming back, underactivity; and two underbound, swelling, merging, overactivity; and holding still, freezing, inactivity. Hitting out is an overactive response; it is overbounded, aggressive, manic, hysterical. Pulling back involves decreasing activity, it is a move away from structure. Freezing and swelling involve lesser degrees of movement.

A somatic process framework is relativistic. Generally, moving out is viewed as assertion while pulling back is not, yet pulling back can be just as assertive as the first. A pulsatory model views moving out and moving back as the same assertive act, only going in different directions. The notion of prepersonal, personal, postpersonal also adds complexity to the framework. The pulsatory system is not rigid and absolute, but is a way to look at clinical phenomena and then deviate safely.

Every structural function, carried to an extreme, invokes its opposite. You see this in a boxer, he organizes and focuses himself to put his power where it belongs. Being out of control is also possible, because in this state he now functions on automatic. But as the focused attack heightens and fear arises, the more frozen or rigid he becomes. He squeezes himself to a point where he becomes unbounded. That is the paradox—one organization, carried to its extreme, becomes the opposite. A client frozen with rage should be moved back a little so that he can contain his rage rather than explode with it. It is the same with a person who pulls back and unbounds himself, if he goes far enough he ends up in primitive contractions, a shrinking state but also a dense one.

Clients reach out to their therapist with their image of who he is or who they need him to be. They will move towards him but may be able to do so only by being aggressive. Reaching out, for them, is threatening. A client may need a response from his therapist that he has never gotten. Therefore he moves towards you in a stiff and rigid way. He also has to deal with your responses. How can he get you back if he needs something? Or another client comes at you in a rigid provoking way in order to agitate you so you will explode and he can then take you in. Or you have a client who says, "uh, uh, uh"—he is unable to speak—and you find yourself rushing in to help him, and discover that he has taken you in.

So the pulsatory continuum involves four movements: expansion, contraction, holding at rest, swelling. We recognize self-extension and swelling as projection and withdrawing and rest as introjection. From there you can arrive at distortions. In expansion or moving out towards the world, there is organization, the creation of form. Withdrawal involves taking back the form, a disorganization. In a homeostatic place there is the maintenance of form. Moving out to the world creates excitatory-emotional energies; moving away from the world involves ingesting the excitatory or emotional energies of others. Staying put means circulating excitatory-emotional states. Excitatory-emotional states, therefore, set the stage for the interaction of bonding.

The following charts illustrate this bonding model:

Chart Two: Pulsation as a Model of the Therapeutic Situation

The child or the prepersonal is unformed, its mother and the society demand form, and the interaction between these two movements creates a third layer, the personal. There is a wave back and forth. In the active fetus there is a normal movement, back and forth, which creates a membrane between what is out there and the fetus. That membrane is the potential separator between the fetus and the world. After birth, this same wave movement continues between raw impulses, the world's reactions to the raw impulses, and the buffer zone. The personality arrives at maturity when it is able to take its involuntary functions and make them voluntary, when it can take its spontaneous, self-programmed, metabolic functions that generate excitement, reach out to the world, reach back in, and regulate its function. This forms a person.

Chart Three: How Boundaries Are Created

Chart Three shows the interactional processes of how membranes become structured, how one goes from a semi-permeable membrane to a less permeable membrane, from having boundaries to a lack of boundaries. The more a person reaches out, the more the world resists, the more membranes are formed. The more the world intrudes, the more he tries to keep the world out, the more membranes he has. The more he moves out, the more he is rejected, the more membranes he makes. At a certain point, if the outer world does not resist and respond to every need, membranes break down or he removes himself and then he has fewer membranes. This is the basic statement of how the distortions of pulsation occur.

CHART TWO:
PULSATION AS A MODEL OF THE
THERAPEUTIC SITUATION

The Outer Pole:
Mother – Society
The Postpersonal

The
Middle
Layer

The
Creation
of a
Boundary

The Inner Pole:
The Child
The Unformed
The Prepersonal
Raw Impulses

The
Personal

The Pulsatory Continuum Between
Mother/Society and the Child Giving
Rise to a Personal Layer

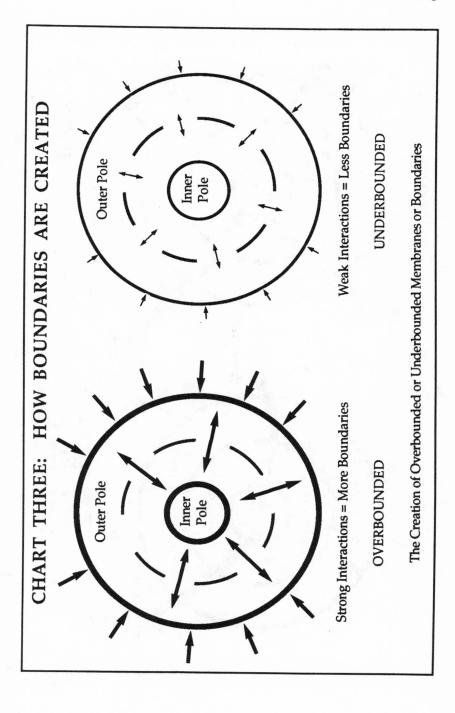

CHART THREE: HOW BOUNDARIES ARE CREATED

Strong Interactions = More Boundaries

OVERBOUNDED

Weak Interactions = Less Boundaries

UNDERBOUNDED

The Creation of Overbounded or Underbounded Membranes or Boundaries

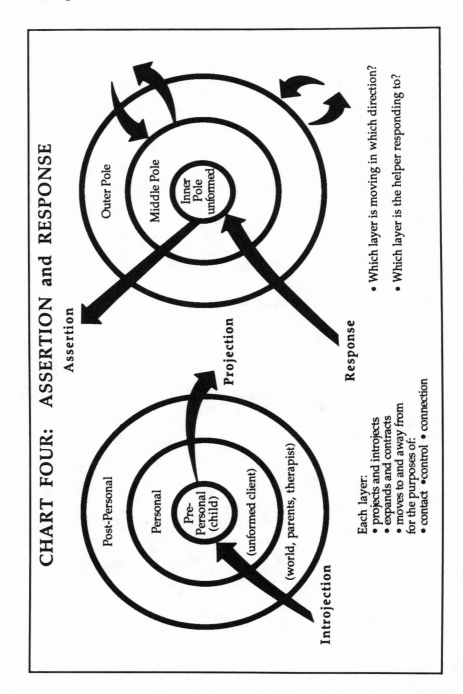

CHART FOUR: ASSERTION and RESPONSE

Assertion

Projection

Response

Outer Pole

Middle Pole

Inner Pole unformed

Post-Personal

Personal

Pre-Personal (child)

(unformed client)

(world, parents, therapist)

Introjection

• Which layer is moving in which direction?
• Which layer is the helper responding to?

Each layer:
• projects and introjects
• expands and contracts
• moves to and away from
for the purposes of:
• contact • control • connection

Chart Four: Assertion and Response

Chart Four shows the basic swelling and congealing movement of reaching out and coming back, swelling and ebbing, opening up and coming back. A person takes his internal state and tries to satisfy it in the outer world. He projects his need onto the outer world and then takes back something that satisfies him from the outer world and withdraws back into himself. This is a normal process, a cyclical process, an ongoing process. A client works with a therapist and projects an organization or a need, and a half-hour later he takes it down and becomes different, only to have the first one return. All of us function on many layers simultaneously. Seeking to form ourselves has to do with the cycling of more mature states to replace less mature states. We are young and old at the same time. For example, a young child tries to act older—he swings back and forth between needing and not needing. This is a normal process. No child perpetually makes his parent into the authority, and no adult continuously wants to be in authority.

In the early part of our lives, a personal self is only a potential, something to become actualized. Basically we swing between the societal world, the outer surface, and the genetic world, the inner world, between the shapes of nature and society. Herd behavior is a good example of society's way. What happens is that there is a need that expands or contracts, moving towards or away from the world, moving from the prepersonal to the societal and back again. It is a two level system with the third just beginning to form or so strongly formed that it acts as a mediator between both worlds. A person has a need to make a connection, to establish continuity, to assert control. Sometimes control comes from the outside. A child wants its parents to act as a mature nervous system even if that control makes the child angry. A child may say, "I want you to give me structure," while behaving in a way that makes the parent give him structure on one of the levels. A therapist works with a client and a flood of involuntary impulses comes to the surface. The client hopes the therapist will offer the structure that permits him to be safely inside that situation yet not infantalized. In the past being out of control meant that the client was helpless; now he does not want to return to that state.

The pulsatory continuum goes from the world to the child, and from the child to the world. By child, in this chart, I mean that relatively unformed part of a client that is looking for the appropriate object to project onto in order to find the responses that encourage him to form. So this chart refers to a young form that is seeking adolescence or adulthood: the novice athlete, to the trained athlete, to the experienced athlete; the young parent, to the growing parent, to the seasoned parent. Moving to the world brings either approval or the rejection that implies the behavior is not appropriate. This chart suggests that therapy deals not with a real child, but with a symbolic form, the infant emerging structure. Of course, not all clients who seek help are underdeveloped children. Some are in crisis because they are in transitions within a relationship. They have an infant-like new identity that does not need to be regressed backwards to solve a parental-child problem which occurred thirty-five years ago. Examples of this might be a person who seeks interdependence rather than independence, or a person whose children are grown, who has a chance to be different in the world, but finds an unformed part of himself that seeks to emerge. The point is that a client's conflict does not always have to do with the past but may have to do with the organization and reorganization of his present form.

Chart Five: Therapeutic Interaction as a Pulsatory Bonding

The basic premise in somatic therapy is that working with a client involves a pulsatory continuum existing on one, two, or three levels— outer, middle, and inner. A therapist interacts on all these three levels with a client. All of the client's layers reach out together or independently. And the therapist responds to the client from one or other of his own layers. For example, a therapist responds from his outer, professional layer to the client's inner deep layer. Or a therapist may go from his societal level to the client's primary process. Or a therapist may use his own primary process to reach the client's primary process through the screen of societal forms. "I will sit behind the couch and comment on your primary process." So the therapist may never interact person-to-person. "I am a screen for this person, I will let him penetrate my societal self while he projects his prepersonal child or his adolescent or childlike adult." Or thousands of other permutations. Or a therapist may have a good relationship with a client and as the contacting waves of the client increase in intensity and go deeper and deeper, the therapist responds with more levels of form, images, and feelings. Which self is the client seeking to project forward and what kind of response does he seek from the therapist? Is the client's prepersonal self seeking a prepersonal response? Is he making the therapist mother or society? What does he need from you? This chart gives a frame of reference to view projection and withdrawal as pulsatory phenomena.

The preceeding charts help the therapist deal with complexity. Since there are so many possible interactions, several understandings are necessary. First, every client is complicated, and the helper has to stand in awe and perhaps confusion at what emerges. Second, it is possible to identify three worlds, inside, middle, outside, as he interacts with you. But, more importantly, this chart demonstrates that contact with a client is a process which leads to an organized behavioral pattern. While many of these processes are semi-automatic or automatic, it is possible for a client to take pieces of them to build his personal life.

If a client does not have boundaries, for example, the therapist has to be a boundary for him until he learns to make his own. That is what external institutions do, they guarantee form. What does a client project onto you? To a client, the therapist may represent the outer pole, mother, father, the other, or all three at once. He puts control onto you, he wants you to control him. Who controls what or do you both control the situation? Or he overcontrols to see how you react. He wants to see how you respond to separation and

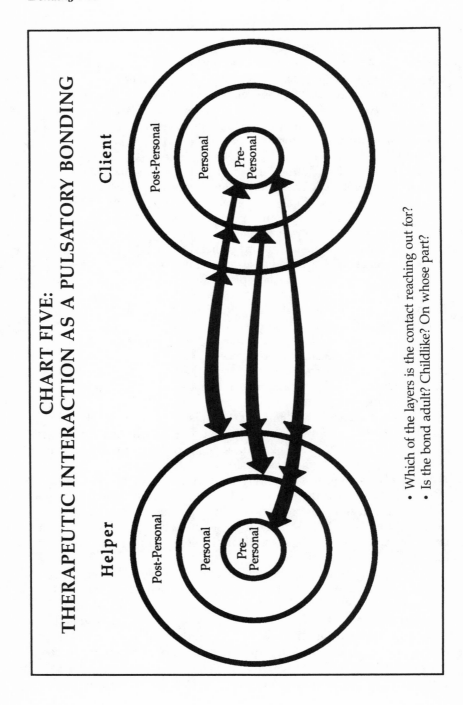

CHART FIVE:
THERAPEUTIC INTERACTION AS A PULSATORY BONDING

Client

Post-Personal

Personal

Pre-Personal

Helper

Post-Personal

Personal

Pre-Personal

• Which of the layers is the contact reaching out for?
• Is the bond adult? Childlike? On whose part?

closeness. Bonding means connection, contact, and control and includes both acceptance and distancing. These charts ask: what is the level of closeness, what is the amount of distance, and who determines either?

There are multiple levels of reality. You may have a client who is adult on the surface but childlike in reality, or a therapist who acts as an adult but is as childlike as the client. What goes on between them is the attempt to establish a pulsatory continuum, one by which they feel their own process of growth or form-making. For most of us, all the levels exist. We are children, and adolescents, and adults. All of us feel this in love-making. We feel the outer surface, the insides, getting closer, the back and forth. So it shouldn't be too hard to remember this same process in a therapeutic interaction.

Remember, the human being functions as a series of organized events, organizing other events. The person is not three pulsating layers. He is an organizing and disorganizing process, a chain of events over time. One session a client will be young, the next time, older. At one moment he is intuitive, then he is back in his dominant, analytical mode. I see it as a symphony of shapes as a client struggles to be with you, trying to organize his behavior in front of you. For example, to say that a rigidly organized person should be more loose, or relaxed is the wrong answer. The question is what is trying to organize or disorganize itself. Is this overbounded person trying to organize an attack or trying to become more receptive?

In this symphony of shapes, there is a shift from one to the other, often very fast. You may say nothing, but only recognize it, and then wait for the right time to address that form. Somatic process sees the self, not as a coherent structure but as parts and pieces circulating around form. Each of us has a consensual shape and dozens of other shapes we assume during the day. Each sends a message about ourselves.

Although Chart Four implies that the three selves are integrated, it is not true. They occupy the same space, they may even talk to each other without knowing it. All of us have a prepersonal self which our personal and societal selves don't understand. We are driven by appetites which force us to do strange things at different parts of the day, like eat, defecate, sleep. But we don't feel those urges in other parts of ourselves. Each part of the organism has little connection to the other, they circulate as separate entities. Our job is to make manifest the connecting shapes. So if someone asks, "who am I" the answer is, "In what realm?" Prepersonally? A replicating machine. Societally? A work unit, part of the tax machine. Constitutionally? A mesomorph-ectomorph according to the categories of William W. Sheldon. Personally? That is what is seeking form.

To sum up, the states described in these charts become manifest when you work somatically, helping people disorganize their chronic contractions and tensions, when you are encouraging excitatory waves, when you are organizing or disorganizing stances. Then clients are much more available. You see the communication between the work that they do on themselves and the place they are in their lives.

The three levels of the client relate, in some way, to the three levels of the therapist. Many times a client hooks into the prepersonal level of the helper because that is where he basically communicates from and the helper has to form a social communication for the client because one doesn't exist. There are other times when the therapist forms a social connection with a client and works the other way. Chart Five suggests what relationship a client wants with the helper. The client may not want integration on all three levels. He may only want to make a relationship between his prepersonal and personal, or bring his prepersonal into the social world. He may not want to form a bond with the helper for more than an hour. He does not want a long-term personal relationship.

How a client bonds with the therapist can also be a model for how he does or does not bond with the world. Unless you know the client in his social environment, all you can describe is how he relates to you in your office and hope that some of it fits. However, you do learn what his prepersonal, personal, and postpersonal states are from watching him do somatic-emotional exercises, or from the language he uses in describing his experience. It would then not be hard to tell a client that he projects onto his boss and makes him a breast to feed off. Further, you can point out why this won't work, or ask why he turns work into a maternal situation.

My personal bias is that the resolution of the intrapsychological dynamics and the one-to-one dynamics manifested in the therapy situation sets the cellular state for a person to relate to the world differently. I don't see the therapist's job as helping a client function more successfully in the world or on his job or making his marriage better. The task is to help the client be with himself in such a way that he forms a life or has some say in the forming of his life. My interest as a somatic therapist is how a client is with himself and how he forms a connection with another person and all the accompanying ingredients.

Every person who exists becomes something, nature programs that. We go from being an embryo to being a fetus, from being a child to becoming an adult, and then we age and die. Of course, families and society and circumstances sometimes stand over us with a baseball bat and make sure we become what they want. But not everyone forms a personal self. Rather the majority of people live lives that are compromises between the prepersonal and postpersonal. And while there is nothing wrong with being in the hands of destiny or God's will, there is also a great deal of wisdom in forming a life.

The therapist asks, "who is this client and what is it he is looking to form?" Does he have a personal relationship with his prepersonal and therefore only wants himself to be lived? When Georg Groddeck formed the concept of the id, he stated that the id lives the ego, the ego is in the service of the id. Freud could not accept that, even though he accepted the concept of the id. Freud said that wherever id is there should ego be. For Groddeck it was the other way around. And the third possibility is wherever ego is, there society should be. It would be the superego at that point. However, I would prefer to be moderately oppressed by society than live in a tribe where nature oppressed me. At least I would know where my three meals were coming from. These are choices.

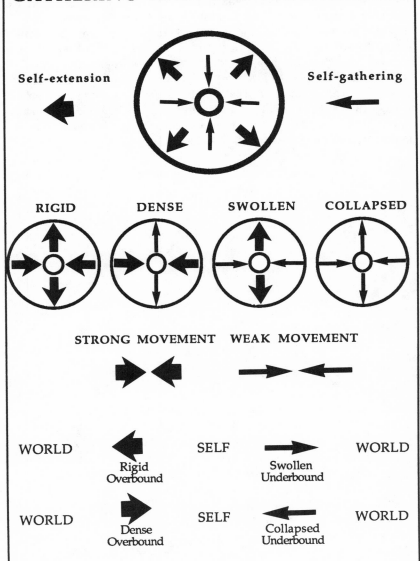

CHART SIX: THE MOVEMENTS OF SELF-EXTENSION AND SELF-GATHERING AND THE DISTORTIONS

Self-extension

Self-gathering

RIGID   DENSE   SWOLLEN   COLLAPSED

STRONG MOVEMENT   WEAK MOVEMENT

WORLD   SELF   WORLD
Rigid
Overbound

Swollen
Underbound

WORLD   SELF   WORLD
Dense
Overbound

Collapsed
Underbound

Chart Six: The Four Movements and their Distortions

Here you see the four movements and their direction: moving toward the world, moving back from the world, resting, and swelling-up in preparation for repeating the cycle. Resting, being inside yourself comes before swelling, the preparation to move towards the world, so it is a cyclical movement. These four forms represent normal movements towards and away from the world and there are four phases to it:

> Expansion into the world, assertion
> Retreating, coming back to yourself
> Rest, containment
> Swelling up, getting ready to act

In the pulsatory continuum, form expresses an intended function. "I want to reach out, I am expanding, I am moving towards the world." "I have had enough, I am retiring, I need to be alone." All of us move towards and penetrate the world. Then we withdraw without retreating from the world and enter a place of moderate repose until we begin to swell with the byproducts of our own metabolism and get ready to act again—four possible movements inside a pulsatory continuum. These four movements have accompanying forms: rigid, dense, swollen and collapsed. Another way to say this is braced, withdrawn, inflated and receptive. With one form we act in the world, in the second we hold our ground, in the third we fill up with ourselves, and in the fourth we create a form whereby we are at ease and receptive. We engage in the world, braced to take on tasks, we retire and withdraw to maintain what we have, we are full of ourselves yet have no need to act, and we discharge and yet feel repose. We have a cycle where we are under-inflated, inflated, holding on to our inflation, then acting on it. A basic rest state, the generation of excitation, the holding of excitation in place, and then acting on it. There are two forms of movement outwards and two forms of movement inward. At this point it is only a continuum of forms; it is not pathological. The two outer layers, acting and holding one's ground, are overbound states, making boundaries, activity. Underbound involves less activity, less boundaries, reposed, at rest.

Pathology enters when there is an inability to disorganize a form, always excited but never allowed to act, charged up and full of potential but without a structure to act. The result is manipulation and seduction, getting others to do it for you. A compulsive, on the other hand, never rests but wins approval through activity, even in sleep he is consciously dreaming.

These are the forms through which a client enters therapy. He may enter therapy in a distorted form, the obsessive person always preparing to act, and making mental categories, like a hunter chasing an animal. You see his activity, stuck in a form, impossible to organize another. What he wants is either for the helper to accept his form, or to challenge it, or to help him change it. "I want you to be the parent who sees I have something good to say." Or "Stay away from me, because if you accept me, I am an adult and therefore I have to take care of myself." The helper may not understand his client's overactivity. Is the adult coming towards the therapist or the child?

In organizing behavior, the client says "I want to be a child in my adult body. Will you, my therapist, let me be a boy? Or do I have to grow up, be an adult, work and not have fun? Do I always have to take care of my family and never be in the position to receive love? Do I only get love for doing a good job?" Or the client says the opposite, "what do you mean, love means taking the other person inside of me? I like my image, I don't want my body to change, I will go out and exercise." So transference is the way a client presents himself to the therapist, the form that he presents to the therapist as well as what he wants in response. The therapist can respond in one of two ways—affirmation or rejection. A therapist doesn't know this at the beginning. But the way a client presents himself gives the therapist a hint about how to respond. Do you confront or act receptive to the rigid and dense ones? Should you let the swollen one get inside you or stop and give them a container to get inside themselves? Do you enter the collapsed person to give them a feeling of structure or make them come out towards you so they build their own structure? These are complicated questions about changing and reorganizing form.

A client moves towards you or you have to move towards him. You have to be confrontive with one and receptive with another. The underbound client sends a message, "I want to be you, or stop me from being you." He needs to enter you in order to re-establish an intrauterine state that was incomplete, for example, borderlines, schizoids. They need a helper to be an accepting uterus. They need to be inside you as a mother. These experiences fill you with awe and humility. You recognize what it is to be consciously in a prepersonal world where the other person reads you like yourself. You feel the circulation of two beings as one. To insist prematurely that the client has no right inside you betrays his rightful expectation. You must take him through the stages of growth and development and sharing and the post uterine experiences where he only sucks instead of taking blood, and so forth. In this way he grows and enters the overbound state.

Then there are overbound clients whom you need to become, where you have to enter them. They have to feel that if someone gets inside them, they won't disappear. If they let another person in them and feel that person, they will learn what empathy and identification with another is. They learn that receiving someone is not humiliation or wipe-out. These people had invasive mothers who entered them and wiped them out. Now anyone who comes close to them is perceived as a danger to the self. Generally, the more rigid and dense forms try to keep the therapist out but you have to enter them, be with them on a primary process level in which there is a circulation of images and free association of ideas, to encourage the pulsatory feeling of being with another without humiliation.

This is what transference means. How do these structural forms affect you? What do they bring out in you? What does the rigid person, the confronter, the inflator and invader, or the retreater bring out in you? A therapist has to organize different forms for different clients. Ultimately, it is how you and the client permit a pulsatory and emotional reality to exist, and how you honestly permit, encourage, or reject the forms that are emerging in him, the kind of person he is struggling to become. If you, as the helper, think a client should be loose as a goose, receive the world, be like Buddha, what do you do with a person who has strong phallic components, one who enjoys attacking the world? Or if you feel like being intuitive and emotional, what do you do with an analytic, rational person? You may want to bring out the inferior function which prohibits him from being more integrated, but not at the expense of over riding his dominant or emerging form.

CHART SEVEN:
THE FOUR MOVEMENTS
AND THEIR DISTORTIONS

		Normal	Distorted
	1st	Expansion Moving Out	Rigid
	2nd	Contraction Moving Back	Dense
	3rd	Rest Containment	Collapse
	4th	Swelling Up Preparation To Act	Swollen

Chart Seven: Self-Extension
and Self-Gathering and their Distortions

A therapist sits with a client and sees the client move towards or away from him while he does the same. The therapist has a societal, an instinctual, and a personal reaction. The client tries to reach towards the therapist in an instinctual way, or share ideas with him, or be in the ambiguity of how to make a personal relationship, something that is neither nature nor society.

All of us have a shape given by nature which gets lived out as our constitutional type. All of us have a shape given by society. We don't exist very long unless we adopt the shape of civility. To do otherwise is to be put away in a mental institution or a prison. Those shapes reflect the tension pattern we try to adopt to get society's acceptance. But all of us also have a personal shape. For some, therapy is viewed primarily as the relationship between societal demands and instinctual demands. "Go back and reconstitute yourself as an animal and then come back and be civilized," is what they say. What I say is that the client has the possibility of being a personalized animal, neither totally in the prepersonal, nor in the societal, nor compromising among them but forming a personal body. While we live in all three worlds, we have the chance to create a personal expression.

How does a client move towards the therapist and how does he move back to himself—that is the question. Every living creature must reach out and come back, even to breathe. This movement of expansion and contraction, to the world and back to the self, is a cyclical event that will manifest itself in the therapeutic encounter. Therapists often impose on therapy statements about how they think they or the client should be. We criticize ourselves for retreating or not being present, rather than taking advantage of how we are present, how we want to retreat and what this means for us. The client says, "Oh, I am not here. How come I am not here, where am I? I'm supposed to be here." Or the countertransference side would be that the helper is "not here." Rather than watching themselves, both sides could talk about how they are or are not present, how they form a bond and then take it down again. Does the client reach out in a strong way or a soft way? Does he try to penetrate you? When does he start to retreat by pulling back? What happens if you, the helper, make a distance? When does he gather back into himself? These are the four types and the four movements— reaching out in a rigid way or in a swollen way, pulling back in a harder way or in a softer way (Chart Seven).

Sexual arousal illustrates the four movements. There is no penetration of the other person unless there is a moderate amount of rigidity. The breasts and the penis have to become erect. The vulva fills out. There has to be a certain amount of organized rigidity to form a channel into the world. After you have organized rigidity to reach out, there is a gradual softening for penetration. You pull back and flow into yourself and become deeply inside in a softer way. So reaching out and coming back involve quantities of rigidity or overboundedness, forming boundaries, or unbounding, taking boundaries down. Accompanying the sexual act are images—penetration; expansive, swollen, incorporating, invading; coming back, defending, holding ground; and sinking into yourself, hibernating, going away.

This chart demonstrates the different ways of reaching out and the shapes of what they look like. The focus is how a client tries to bond with you. This is what transference is all about. If he wants to form a bond with you in a rigid way, do you want to soften his rigidity prematurely? Or if he tries to hold his ground, do you try to break it down? Or if he wants to retreat from you, do you have to chase him and tell him he is not in contact? These are the questions to ask.

Chart Eight: The Bonding of the Four Types

Every client wants, in some way or other, to have the courage to enter your office in all the ways that are truthful to himself in the moment and then find ways to withdraw. During a session you can see when the client starts to withdraw. Often he compensates not to let it end, for example, by talking more. The observation is not that the client talks more but how he tries to interrupt the therapist's withdrawal.

The basic statement is that every person seeks to be master of the form of the relationship. A sense of mastery was denied the client in the past and is what needs to be defended in the present. Every person has this basic conflict—how is he going to form or not form the relationship he is in. He wants to have a sense of continuity and control in his life whether he asks to be understood or challenged. The basic theme is the emergence of how form tries to concretize or dissolve itself.

A person seeks to have control, contact, and connection with his own process. The ticklish part of this is that some people can only do that through others. They can only have control, contact, and continuity with themselves by accepting the form of others or getting others to give them form. When I was in training in Zurich, Medard Boss said "There are two kinds of birds, a whole flock of birds sitting together and over there a lone bird. One of the flock flies away and the whole flock follows, but the one bird still sits." So there are birds who need contact and birds who need to be alone. Likewise, some people like being in the herd, but others need a relationship to the herd that is slightly distant.

Trying to control a situation and trying to control your own insides are somewhat similar. There are as many people who try to change their outside world as there are others who try to change their internal world in relation to the outside. These are choices, constitutional and psychological choices. If you change your internal state you also change your external state.

Chart Eight continues to define the notion of projection and introjection. A client takes his internal state, which represents his urges, and thrusts it towards the world. He projects onto the environment what has to be there for him to function. Any movement towards the world carries with it a whole series of projections and assumptions. When you dismantle a client's defensive structure, when you encourage a person to move a certain way, breathe a certain way, exercise in a certain way, you set up an indirect challenge to his structure. This challenge stokes the fires and creates images and urges that begin to move towards the world. The client's projection

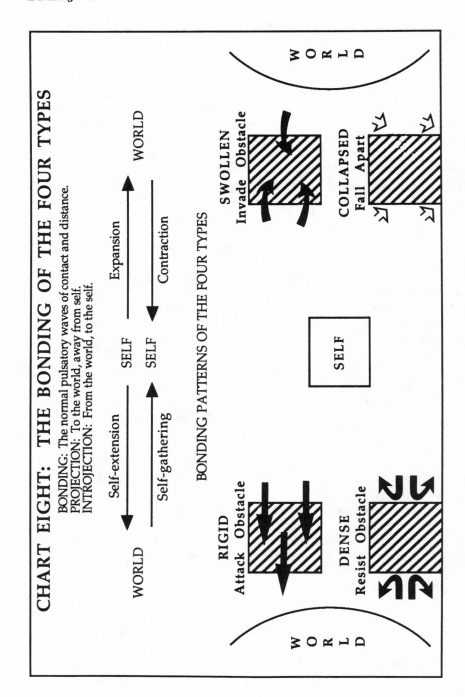

CHART EIGHT: THE BONDING OF THE FOUR TYPES

BONDING: The normal pulsatory waves of contact and distance.
PROJECTION: To the world, away from self.
INTROJECTION: From the world, to the self.

WORLD ← Self-extension → SELF
WORLD ← Self-gathering → SELF

WORLD ← Expansion → SELF
SELF ← Contraction → WORLD

BONDING PATTERNS OF THE FOUR TYPES

SELF

RIGID
Attack Obstacle

DENSE
Resist Obstacle

SWOLLEN
Invade Obstacle

COLLAPSED
Fall Apart

W O R L D

W O R L D

may not get as far as the world, it may only get to his surface screen, but it will still be a movement outwards towards the world and a movement backwards towards his internalized world.

The pulsatory model of contact and distance shows that it is impossible to be in the world without the other. Chart Eight shows movement towards the world and the projection of internal states, needs, and memories upon the world, hoping for a certain kind of response. A client who had no father seeks a father in every man he meets. He projects onto the other a fatherly response and becomes disappointed when he does not get it.

Every impulse that arises in a person seeks a parental environment in its initial stages. For example, someone recently gave me a mask so I became interested in learning about masks. I thought of going to the library and getting a book out, but then decided to talk to a friend who knows about masks. With this projection I made the first boundary. I wanted a response to something that was new, so I sought, in the guise of information, a more experienced body. It would be inappropriate if I merely followed an authority down the line rather than introjecting the dialogue for the growth of my interest.

Chart Eight shows the client moving towards the world and back to himself. Self-gathering and self-extension, expansion and withdrawal. These are different terms for the same phenomenon depending upon the client's level of organization. If he lives on the prepersonal level, he merely expands and contracts; if he has some societal role or personal self, then he moves towards society or a personal self. The bottom of the chart points out what happens when different types of clients meet an obstacle or a challenge. The rigid will attack it, try to knock it down. The swollen will invade and surround it. The dense will withdraw from it. The weak will collapse under it. This is the normal expansion and contraction cycle and how it organizes ways to get to the world or away from the world. The images of rigid and swollen seem somewhat the same but they differ. To understand the difference, imagine being seduced. Someone moves towards you in a very assertive way and swallows you up. But they haven't swallowed you, they have invaded you. It is different from a punch in the nose. It is like the old saying, "the object of war is not to win but to get your own way."

The therapist asks the question, how is a client trying to get close, how is he trying to form a bond? How does the therapist respond? Does he insist on his own way? Some people make contact vigorously. Others implant surreptitiously. Some invite you in while others resist. There are clients that like to argue, those that like to fight, those that like to let you bounce against them, those that let you in so they can assimilate you, and those that like to surround and invade you.

The inner life is similar, an internal dance that goes on among the social, the prepersonal, and the personal. Many times the inner conflict between the prepersonal and the personal is projected outwardly onto the world. The dialogue between forming a relationship with the personal self and the instinctual self is lived out by demanding that another take the role of your own internal life. "I cannot control myself, you please control me. I am overwhelmed by my own internal processes, you please be my adult. I have a personal need to give myself over to my prepersonal but I do so by fusing myself to your sensations. I cannot be my own adult but I can be yours. I cannot rigidify myself but I can get you to, therefore I live through you what I cannot in myself." Or the collapsed person, "I can't form a boundary or an internal structure so I will get you to do it."

Lecture Four

Dismantling the Bond

Somatic process work looks at how a client has structured his
past experience and how he can destructure it to form a new structure. When a client's way of reaching out and coming back to himself
is thwarted, his form gets repressed or distorted. Then he projects
his needs onto the world in stylized ways. A central focus of somatic
process work is disorganizing these muscular-emotional patterns.
This is called grounding, a somatic, psychological, and emotional
process which involves imagination, thought, feeling, and action.

The relationships a client has had with significant others in his
infancy, childhood, and adolescence determine the closeness or
distance of his bond with his therapist. A therapist notices this by
how a client comes close to him or pushes him away, how he invades
him, pushes in, remains aloof, clings to him, or refuses to let go.
These are muscular-emotional patterns: a sunken, defeated chest, a
pulled-back jaw, stiff-necked caution, an agitated pelvis, a fearful
sucked-up belly, or angry hunched shoulders. Different patterns may
indicate expectations of rejection or humiliation. The client may
wish to fight with his therapist or to please him. The client's historical
past is present as he expects the therapist to argue with him,
humiliate him, be subservient or reject him, meet his every need, be
kind, or take care of him when he feels childlike. This transference
of the past onto the present is, certainly, the first step in trying
to establish contact as one has known it.

A somatic therapist helps a client by utilizing the Five Steps
(*Embodying Experience*, Center Press, 1987). The client's dependencies, terrors, hidden fears, and humiliations are expressed in the
shape of his body. This somatic-emotional expression is Step One, its
organization Step Two. Step Three is how a client disorganizes his
structure. The incubation of feelings, associations, insights is Step
Four, and his urge toward new organization is Step Five.

The Five Steps

Step One: The client's story, his situation, the way he attempts to bond to the therapist, his chronic behavior, his habitual role.

Step Two: How the client organizes muscularly and emotionally his story, situation, bond, behavior, and role.

Step Three: How the client disorganizes the somatic and emotional expression of his story, situation, bond, behavior, and role.

Step Four: How the client deals with the nonvolitional rise of associations, past memories, and feelings.

Step Five: How the client uses himself to establish a new story, bond, situation, behavior and role.

Each of these steps is accompanied by certain feelings and thoughts. Will I be successful in constructing my role and performing? Will I be rejected if I don't construct my role and can't or won't perform? Will I be abandoned, alienated or left alone if I take a long time to reform? Can I bear the unknown as I try to reform? Therapists, likewise, respond to these different stages in their own way. They may get anxious, rejecting, cautious or over-identified with any of the stages, desire, organization, disorganization, association and feeling, and re-forming.

The stages of how a client bonds to a therapist can be reorganized. In seeking emotional and developmental growth and contact, the client moves towards and away from the therapist. He bonds and makes contact, then disorganizes to make a different contact. Through this process he learns closeness and distance and how to sustain and interrupt contact, continuity, and control. When a therapist participates in the process of undoing the way a client bonds with him, the client's need for closeness and support remains high. Fears of aloneness or abandonment may arise until the client learns to manage the storms of excitement and emotion that threaten his organismic integrity. A client asks for responsiveness and when given, it helps the client form independence.

Bonding and reorganizing the bond requires the therapist and client to learn how they function, to exploit their past emotional experiences and associations, and to learn the skills of self-management and control. The Five Steps provide a structure for this learning.

The Five Steps: Somatizing the Bond

STEP ONE: I ask a client to describe his somatic posture in relation to me, for example, being submissive or braced to fight or trying to please me. He may discover that his psychological placation involves the muscular organization of stiffening his neck and smiling, or puffing-up his chest, a psychological stance of exaggerated bravery or sexuality. He begins to recognize STEP TWO, his pattern of muscular contractions. He sees how these are connected to memories, associations, and feelings of past hurts in which he needed to defend himself muscularly and psychologically. He recognizes how he is fused or embedded in his story of hurt and disappointment and how he projects the need of the past onto the present, making the therapist a fearful or accepting authority.

When challenged to disorganize this pattern by slowly taking apart its emotional-muscular organization, STEP THREE, the client begins to feel his fear of being without structure. He may remember past terror or helplessness and feel it internalized inside. Separation and disorganization help create a distance from what has been internalized and split off from self-knowledge. For example, the stiff neck of placation hides the feelings of terror associated with another's rejection. At STEP THREE, disorganization, the terror is transferred onto the therapist who is asked not to act as the parents or authorities did in the past. Furthermore, the client's helplessness may yield to anger or crying. As a therapist, you manage your own reaction to the client's terror, helplessness, anger or tears and try to teach him that disorganization need not be associated with past helplessness. Then he can learn to live with his emotional disorganization.

When internalized forms of past bonding are disorganized, the client enters a stage of unformedness, STEP FOUR. Here past images and feelings incubate and the client learns to integrate the lessons of his pain differently. This place of emotional-muscular-psychological restoration gives rise to the feelings and insights that enable a client to make another type of bond with significant people, STEP FIVE. This step demands a responsive and interactive attitude on the part of the therapist. Forming a new bond is not only an act of imagination or feeling. It involves the ways a client practices using his brain and muscles to integrate emotional, imaginative learning into a connection for contact he can control or manage.

This Five Step process of bonding, dismantling the bond, and rebonding is a pulsatory pattern of expansion and contraction, organization and disorganization. It is similar to the embryo changing form at two hundred and eighty days, or a child's learning to bond with his mother and then changing that bond to grow into adolescence and adulthood. We all bond and dismantle bonds many times—as an embryo, infant, child, adolescent, adult, with old age, and death. Pulsating between poles of existence involves bonding and the changing of bonds and is what a therapist sees as his clients try to relive these stages and recognize and form the feelings that have split off. The Five Steps contain the scope of human experiencing, the basic process of how we internalize the world and then project it outward. In this process we grow our own shape. When a client can accept that in any given situation his own self comes to the surface, he no longer is afraid of his life or whatever life brings him. That is a major goal of doing somatic therapy.

The therapist aligns with the Five Steps, what is the client's story or situation, how does he organize it, how is he going to disorganize it, what will happen if he does nothing, and how is he going to use these experiences to rebond again. The concerns of a somatically-oriented helper are how a client exaggerates his situation, how he destructures this exaggeration, how he rests in the tidepools, and how he organizes to come out again with his insights. These are the Five Steps.

The Five Steps are the way a client embodies his experience and destructures his past. The helper joins with the client to destructure his past experience or to organize a structure for his present experiences even though his past is involved. Establishing and dismantling bonds has to do with organizing an identity. To best understand a client a therapist should ask whether he is disorganizing, maintaining, or reorganizing a form.

The Emergence of Unresolved Feelings

In working with clients in somatic-emotional process, once deep structures of defense are dismantled, emotions will surface. The pulsatory rhythm of bonding and unbonding involves projection and introjection, expanding an internal state into the world or pulling back into one's self. This rhythm may be accompanied by feelings of fear and anger, grief and sadness. With expansion, a client fears losing himself; with contraction he fears losing his connection to his therapist. Both situations arouse the client's fear of losing his boundaries. Another fear is invoked by projecting outward or taking in. A client imagines the dangers of penetration, another being inside him, or being in the unknown. Another fear is absorbing the therapist. These cases involve the fear of losing what is.

The reverse is equally true. Asking a client to contract his muscles may bring anger and feelings of loss from having to reduce himself as well as the fear of becoming smaller. Another client will maintain frantic activity so that he never shrinks, or gets small, or comes back from the world to his inflated self. Still another client inhibits every excitatory emotional swelling so as to refrain from being unbounded.

Clients try to inhibit or exaggerate the normal tidal process of expansion, swelling, assertion, or contraction, self-gathering, withdrawal. Either they swell up with themselves, get rigid or dense to prevent shrinking, or get dense or sink in to prevent expansion.

How a client bonds with a therapist is directly related to the way that client experiences his own patterns of expansion and contraction. A collapsed type undermines his own expansion from inside out; his impulses and desires never swell up. He accuses the therapist either of not understanding him or he seeks excessive support. The helper feels restrained or aggressive as his efforts are swallowed up or unresponded to.

The swollen client is overly expansive, verbally assertive, and never retreats back into himself. He takes every one of the helper's impulses and deflects them with manic-like associations and verbiage. The helper feels he is defending himself against an excitatory, emotional flood. An individual with this structure carries on the same type of warfare internally. He overwhelms himself, he is always in a flood or turmoil, every impulse must be lived out. This behavior forces his therapist to act as a dam, a policeman, or a boundary-maker.

The rigid client transfers authority onto the therapist so he can then try to break him down with his assertion. In this situation, internal arousal overwhelms the rigid's internal structures either by fragmenting him or blowing him out with excuses and persuasion. He projects everything onto the helper who becomes overwhelmed or restrictive or tries to be reality to the person. The function of the projection is to make the therapist a boundary for the client.

The dense client crushes every impulse in himself so he is perpetually depressed, never internally aroused, never allowing hope to arise. This self-compacter uses an image of internal criticism to perpetuate his internal shrinking, attacking himself, or discouraging himself. The therapist becomes his savior, the reservoir of hope, the known boundary. Individuals with this structure project a need for containment, boundaries, acceptance and hope to be rescued without humiliation. As different types of clients go through the Five Steps, they call out for response to their organization and disorganization and the therapist's responses should be consistent with the client's pattern of expansion and contraction.

Practical Applications and Methodology

The following questions review the pulsatory model of bonding and the Five Steps. They are intended to help a therapist explore the nature of the bond that both he and the client establish.

The Nature of the Bond

1) What is the nature or the image of the bond?

2) What are the actions the client takes to maintain this bond?

3) How can a client inhibit, undo, or disorganize his muscular-emotional pattern of bonding?

4) How does a client allow the upwelling of fresh response and insights?

5) How does he use himself to organize new emotional- psychological insights into action?

Bonding and the Five Steps

1) How does the client present himself? (what bond is he attempting to relive)

2) What roles or actions are organized?

3) How are they disorganized? (inhibition of action and story)

4) How does the client accept undifferentiation? (free association of images, feelings)

5) How does the client reform his bond?

The Bonding Situation

1) What is the developmental state of the client? (uterine, maternal, incestuous, oedipal, rejection, fear, ambivalence, acceptance, confusion, safety)

2) How is his bond organized? (fused, united, polarized, undifferentiated, close, differentiated)

3) How is his bond dismantled? (distance, separation, severance)

4) How does the client live without bonds? (immersed, abandoned, exiled, undifferentiated, creative, free-flowing, incubated)

5) How does the rebonding occur?

The Bond Between Client and Therapist

The Five Steps can be used to understand the form of bonding between therapist and client:

From the view of the client:

1) How does he form an image of bonding? (son, daughter, friend, student)

2) How does he somatically organize this bond?

3) What happens when he disorganizes this bond?

4) How does he envision a new form of bond?

5) He does he maintain this new bond?

From the view of the therapist:

1) What is your image of bonding as a therapist? How do you receive the client? (father-mother)

2) What roles or actions do you perform to perpetuate this bond?

3) How do you withdraw, inhibit, disorganize from these roles or actions?

4) How do you wait and create a new vision or intuition of the bond?

5) How do you reorganize or create a new form of bonding?

The Four Types

The Client's Basic Therapeutic Stance

In working with a client, central questions to explore are the nature of his somatic form, what function it serves in relationship to the therapist, and how you, the therapist, respond to the different types.

Rigid: makes a form to keep the therapist from entering by attacking, penetrating or appeasing him. The function is to be separate, fragmenting others yet remaining agitated. Independence is the goal.

Dense: makes a form to ward the therapist off, resists entrance, withdraws from the field of action, alternately provokes and resists. Nothing gets in or out. Accumulates energies to erupt. Freedom is the goal.

Swollen: makes a form to get into the therapist, flatters to take in or incorporate the therapist or get invited in by being what the therapist wants, seduces, mimics to make bonding possible. The goal is containment.

Collapsed: makes a form to arouse the therapist, the function is to be rescued, to avoid effort, or to delay commitment. Mobilizes the therapist's empathy and support to get structure. The goal is inflation.

The Bonding Sequence

The bonding sequence is different for the four types:

1) Hunger for contact

2) Actions towards it, directly or indirectly:
   Rigid-fight   Swollen-hope
   Dense-hold back   Collapsed-grab

3) Actions away from contact, inhibition:
   Rigid-go around   Swollen-wait
   Dense-put off   Collapsed-passive

4) Behavior after, during contact:
   Rigid-seeks distance   Swollen-seeks closeness
   Dense-seeks distance   Collapsed-seeks closeness

5) Change

The Characteristic Patterns of the Four Types

One: The client's hungers and needs.

Two: How a client reaches out or projects
Rigid: assertively
Dense: eruptively
Swollen: impulsively
Collapsed: cautiously

Three: How the client pulls back or introjects
Rigid: through resisting
Dense: by erupting
Swollen: by oozing back
Collapsed: by giving in

Four: How a client waits in an unbounded state
Rigid: by agitation
Dense: through determination
Swollen: with impatience
Collapsed: in resignation

Five: How the client comes back to the world is open-ended. A client may return to his original structure in order to perfect his past or he may organize less rigidity, density, swollenness, collapse.

Each stage has its own accompanying demand upon the therapist. Does the client want his therapist to respond to him in a way that supports Stage Two or supports Stage Three? Does he present the helper with his Stage Two rigidity, organization, projection, penetration of the world and want the therapist to receive him or resist him? Does he want to be received so as to feel the power of Two to enter Three or does he want his therapist to resist him so as to feel the power of Two or pull back and feel the power of Three? Does he want the helper to accompany and be with him in Stage Four where he free-floats back and forth or does he want the therapist to be the container which he swims in to feel contained before he emerges? Should the therapist kick him out or let him find a way out?

The Function of Bonding

Bonding is how a client maintains connection, contact, and continuity. It is how he exercises control over his closeness and distance to the other. A client may force himself on others (rigid/swollen) or stay away from them (dense/collapsed). Rigid and dense types are self-centered and excessively demanding. Swollen and collapsed types are borderlines, they wish to be the other.

> The rigid person projects domination or war with authority.
> The dense person projects being invaded, too many demands.
> The swollen person wishes to be the other.
> The collapsed person wishes you to be inside them.

Does This Client Have Difficulties

> In seeking support?
> In letting another enter him without being humiliated?
> In entering another without losing himself?
> In resisting another without eruption?
> In dominating a situation without hostility?
> In being submissive?
> In being passive?
> In being receptive?
> In being dominant?
> In withdrawing?
> In controlling?
> In identifying with others?
> In acting on long-term goals?
> In acting on frustration?
> In being faithful to a vision?

The Excitatory Pattern of the Client

In working with a client, the essential question to ask concerns the quality of his vitality, desire, and aliveness (high, moderate, low) and its direction (inward or outward). Which needs to be disorganized and reorganized?

Rigid: high vitality, directed outward. The rigid wants to get into his therapist but fears the opposite.

Dense: low vitality, directed inward. The dense wants to keep his therapist out to avoid being accepted.

Swollen: high vitality, directed outward. The swollen wants to merge with his therapist.

Collapsed: low vitality, directed inward. The collapsed wants his therapist to become part of him.

Therapeutic Methodology

Therapists utilize a variety of techniques and methodologies in working with their clients. From a somatic-emotional perspective, the question to ask of each of these methodologies is:

Does it structure a client?
Does it destructure a client?
Does it create a free-floating state for the client?
Does it create withdrawal for the client?

Countertransference Traps

A therapist can be trapped by the strengths and limitations of his own somatic structure. Some of the areas to be alert to are:

Rigid: pushes client to move, overcome his resistance, yet resists affection coming from client.

Dense: little push towards action, settles for recognition acceptance, empathy; resists client's attack.

Swollen: over-identifies with client, identifies with client's internal state, pushes to control events.

Collapsed: withdraws from contact, resists affection or action.

Rigid and swollen therapists tend to keep the client distant; domination is the central issue.

Dense and collapsed therapists try to get the client close; contact and connection are the issues.

Therapist-Client Bondings by Type

Listed below are possible therapist-client interactions based on the structure of both the therapist and the client.

	THERAPIST'S POSITION	CLIENT'S POSITION
Rigid	Action orientation, confrontation, attack, association	I'll do it my way
Dense	Provokes client, encourages client to come out, frustrates, empathizes with	I won't Leave me alone
Swollen	Tries to get in, incorporates, encourages	Be me
Collapsed	Tries to get client inside them, empathizes, identifies with	Help me

The Five Steps Contrasted to the Four Types

Each client, depending on his structure, will find one or the other of the Five Steps difficult or easy.

FIVE STEPS	TYPES STRONG IN THIS AREA	TYPES WEAK IN THIS AREA
1) Image, situation, recognition of reality (embedded, at a distance, polarized, collapsed)		
2) Organization; action (Forming boundaries)	Rigid, Dense	Swollen, Collapsed
3) Disorganization (Unforming boundaries)	Collapsed	Rigid, Dense, Swollen
4) Creation, incubation (Living with minimal form)	Swollen, Collapsed	Rigid, Dense
5) Reorganization, re-forming	Rigid	Dense, Swollen Collapsed

Countertransference Questions

What is your therapeutic response to each of the types as:

image
structure
feeling
action

How do you respond:

To attack, invasion, penetration?
To resistance, rebellion, being kept out?
To incorporation?
To being inhabited, asked for support?

Potential Bonding Roles Based on Therapist-Client Gender

MALE THERAPIST	FEMALE CLIENT	MALE CLIENT	FEMALE THERAPIST
FATHER	MOTHER	FATHER	MOTHER
ADULT MALE	ADULT FEMALE	ADULT MALE	ADULT FEMALE
SON	DAUGHTER	SON	DAUGHTER
BROTHER	SISTER	BROTHER	SISTER
BOY	GIRL	BOY	GIRL

MALE THERAPIST	MALE CLIENT	FEMALE CLIENT	FEMALE THERAPIST
FATHER	FATHER	MOTHER	MOTHER
ADULT MALE	ADULT MALE	ADULT FEMALE	ADULT FEMALE
SON	SON	DAUGHTER	DAUGHTER
BROTHER	BROTHER	SISTER	SISTERS
BOY	BOY	GIRL	GIRL

Which of these roles are you capable of taking as:
     a male therapist?
     a female therapist?

Which of these roles is your client capable of taking as:
     a male client?
     a female client?

Bond client desires: ----------------------------------➤

Bond therapist permits: --------------------------------➤

Ann:
To Bond as a Young Woman or as a Child

Therapist: I would like to present a client of mine whom I have difficulties with.

Ann is a woman in her second marriage, with two children. She works as a sales clerk. Her original complaints were a lack of emotional support and having to answer everyone's demands. Even though she felt inadequate, she had to return to work because of financial demands. There was a cycle to her behavior, she would get a job, start to work adequately, experience increasing pressure to do more, collapse and become ill, take off sick days, then quit or be fired. This happened over and over. She had numerous somatic complaints: asthma, migraine, neck and shoulder pains, vaginal infections, and abdominal pains.

She was born in New York and lived with both her parents. She remembers wanting to take drama lessons but her parents prevented it. Her parents worked so she sought out the neighbors for companionship for which she was reprimanded. She also had to care for her brother. She was constantly told by her parents that she was inadequate. Her story is one of rejection. Her first marriage was to escape her parents but the man she married had a major illness and after his recovery Ann divorced him. She had a number of jobs and, as an escape, had a promiscuous life style. She began visiting doctors for the complaints listed before. She began to use an antidepressant. Her second husband, like her father, was a college graduate who turned down better paying jobs for manual labor. This is when she came to therapy.

Let me give you an example of the crisis Ann lives in. Her mother was ill and wanted to come and live with Ann even though Ann's husband wasn't working. Ann didn't want her mother to come, yet also felt angry and guilty about it. She didn't want to take care of her mother, yet feared she would capitulate.

Stanley Keleman: What is the problem so far? Your presentation is too general, not precise enough.

T: She originally came for a few sessions and that was several years ago. Then, she wanted me to be accepting and nonrejecting. But, now, maybe she is ready for a different type of therapy. Perhaps she needs a different response from me. I would like to show you a picture she made of herself.

S.K: This somagram presents a form that is collapsed, withdrawn, and swollen. The legs, arms, and head are weak. It looks like a woman sticking her head out of the undifferentiated world of primary process. There is little oxygenation. This person is struggling.
Let us use the Five Steps. Step One is the somagram as well as the story you have presented. Ann's story, Step One, is, "I am a woman who could have made it but I was undermined in my independence." But her somagram shows a woman who cannot act. So her story and her image are different. We are looking at potential without form. A further part of her story is "I couldn't because of them, but maybe, because of you, I can." Her physical symptoms are a disorganizing pattern involving protest, anger, calls for help, withdrawal, and collapse. Ann is asking for support, asking you to fill her, keep her active, lift her depression.

The impasse you feel as her therapist has to do with the kind of bond the two of you have formed over the past few years. Given that this client has deep, early longing for support and recognition, she needs mothering. She sought a mouth-breast connection and you gave one to her. You both sense that a new form wants to emerge in her now. It appears from the story you tell of her that she wants to be more assertive, more separate. She is asking to become more independent. Her physical shape, however, does not have the struc-ture to support this. Your helplessness has to do with the support you give her which does not encourage fully her somatic assertiveness and boundary formation. You encourage her verbally but not somati-cally. Your continuation of what was previously required, the umbilical-mother-breast role, does not give Ann the feelings of physical strength and separation which she now requires. Maybe you need to help her practice what the relationship could be rather than what it should be. Maybe you can help her to withstand more pressure. Ann has to learn somatic-emotional firmness and separation. She has to feel both distance and closeness as nonthreatening. She has to say no when she feels too many demands and begin to say yes to herself. In this way she can organize her sense of reality. Clearly she does not know how to form or manage her assertion. Her somagrams show a submissive woman who lacks self-esteem. You also see a child, a fearful child, a frozen adolescent. And her parental reality told her "you are inadequate, you should be obedient, and not assertive."

So Ann is emotionally conflicted between the child in her and her attempts at adulthood. She fears having to fulfill the demands of others, yet she also fears abandonment. She needs to separate from the breast and demand that her therapist treat her as older. It is not enough for you to be a uterus or a breast. You have to encourage her to use herself to be more assertive and control her own collapse. This would give her a better sense of her reality, starting with her own assertive stance. We know that she can work, we also know that she protests through collapse. Now her therapist has to provide Ann with body firmness and approve those actions she takes for herself rather than for others.

You could make a contract with Ann that from now on you are not going to be so accepting as a parent, you will be much more an older sibling or a shaper of her female self. You could tell her, " You are an adult and you have to use your chest, starting with breathing. That is your exercise. I insist that you tell me about breathing and feelings in the chest and the kinds of anxiety or excitement you get from your chest when you are with others. Because if you continue not breathing, or being assertive in the chest you will continue to get asthma attacks and not have enough energy, and other people will use your fear to dominate you. You must begin to give your self an asserting form."

Now the question is why you, the therapist, do not show her how to use her chest or be more assertive with you. Why do you empathize with her frightened little child? Why do you not see her retreat as a statement of aggression as well as defeat? Do you not see her collapse as a demand for you to come to her or a fear that her assertion will be rejected by you?

A formative somatic-emotional approach would also include a sexual history. For example, "what did it mean to have your period or how were you as a teenager around your erotic impulses?" In this way you would get a hint of how she tried to use herself in the world and form her adolescence. She might get a hint of how to be in the world more as a female and dismantle the dowdy woman. And then you might get closer to her middle layer. You may be responding to a middle-aged woman which is true for her outside and her frozen inner child but it is not true for her unformed adolescent young woman. You are in the position where she doesn't know how to bring her active young lady to the foreground, and you, then, are just like her parents. There may be a hibernation hiding behind the collapsed chest. You could ask her, "what do you think wants to come out and form itself." Pay attention to that over and over. Ask her to contract and relax her chest. Undo the hiding. This is Stage Three. Then a dream, a fantasy, a forgotten wish may come to the surface to be practiced somatically, Stage Four. But her somagram suggests that you would be defeated if you lifted her expectations too high on the ladder of performance. That means you have to grow up a young, older woman. The somatic-emotional exercise, then, is for Ann to use herself, to form her young woman by practicing lifting the chest and exhaling with demand and eros. Her statement then becomes, "Here I am, appreciate me, don't make me into a dowdy adult."

If you look at her picture you see a dense, overbounded, crushed chest and a swollen, weak, passive lower body. The organs of vitality and love have been squelched while the organs of gender and sexuality are unformed Her efforts keep her infantalized, a servant, asexual, and results in failure. She ends up feeling she is "not good enough" and then, probably, projects that onto you. This bond should be dismantled. Your major effort is to disorganize the "not good enough."

The essential goal of somatic process work is for a person to experience his life in its bodily and emotional shape with the feelings that are present and how they are organized, and then to know the associated meanings and memories. To know your own forming process is to know how you have embodied experience.

What is the meaning of failure for Ann? Is it a rebuke to her parents, is it a statement of not knowing how to form the next stage, or a statement about receiving too many demands? Is Ann saying, "Let me grow for myself according to my own standards?" If your stance as her therapist is only to be supportive or to avoid confrontation, then the client's emerging form meets mush and her somatic reality will be undermined. Maybe you have to be more firm yet not demanding of her. In this situation Ann's collapse and unboundedness is a retreat from her parent's reality and a search for her own. You have supported her as a womb and a breast. Now you could respond to her demands by teaching her the physicality of being assertive and self-supporting. Dismantling the mouth-breast connection will allow the genital connection to emerge where there is individuality and separateness. Then Ann can learn her reality by trial and error rather than by others defining her reality.

Now let us look at how you are connected to her. You bond with Ann in a soft, supportive, encompassing, nurturing connection. Connection and contact are given high priority but not control. Ann is now calling for this bond to change. You mentioned that her marriages involved men who were too demanding and who made her support them. It strikes me that she has competence yet collapses under duress and stress. Scoliosis, asthma, migraines, depression are statements of conflict around assertion. She needs support for her protest. She is an unformed adolescent, marginally functioning, yet she can work and meet reality demands, only not for herself.

I would like to ask why you respond in such a cautious way to this kind of person? Can you present her a surface to bounce off of? Does your own softness and laid-back stance make a statement about not arousing or upsetting the woman? Is your bond saying, "don't be more than I can handle somatically?

T: My father taught me not to upset my mother as she was sick and complaining. Given her history she could not accept aggressive or obstreperous behavior. I tried to harmonize and please her.

S.K: How do you do that?

T: I draw back, don't confront, don't use vigorous statements or inflame the situation.

S.K: Does a vigorous stance or presenting yourself as pushing back mean the woman may sense that she is being challenged?

T: What do you mean?

S.K: Well, it seems to me that scoliosis, asthma, vaginal-abdominal pain are a statement about conflict in the organs of excitation and longing for self-definition as well as for support for herself as a woman. Your client collapses but is capable of acting independently, only not as a woman.

T: My mother was sickly and demanding. She didn't want the family to be any trouble. Even my father placated her. I must say that I don't wish to be angry with my client. I also don't want her to make more demands of me.

S.K: Your client uses anxiety to break out of her mouth-breast connection to you. Her life history is that her own sense of reality is downgraded. Now she wishes to bond with you in a way that is more assertive. All of her physical symptoms are statements about the conflict between assertion-independence and compliant-subservience. Is the anti-depressant an attempt to quell the anxiety and excitement of self-assertion? Is this not the same as the compression and collapse of Ann's chest diminishing the rise of her excitation?

Your own unwillingness to be more forceful reveals the problem. By viewing her as an older woman who needs help, you create a stance of overprotection, something you are familiar with from your own past. What I am suggesting is that the mouth-breast bond has ended and you need to bring the next level into play by becoming more assertive. You could begin by asking Ann how you affect her. Get her to talk about how she experiences you.

T: I see, I should try to act more firmly.

S.K: I mean try giving yourself a firm look, brace yourself, begin to undo the overprotective state you have as well as present a more vivid picture of the situation.

T: That means to breathe more in my chest.

S.K: That is correct.

T: I see that I don't breathe much in my chest as it makes me anxious.

S.K: About what?

T: I feel I would shout: "Don't be so damn weak. I am sick of your lack of excitation."

S.K: I would imagine that your own chest feelings are projected onto your client.

T: Maybe the concern with feeling my own excitement and protest keeps my chest repressed.

S.K: Maybe now that you have begun Step Three, to undo your chest, you can sense its meaning—don't be excited or angry around mother, don't be bad. So we have Step One, your laid-back, protective, caring stance. And, Step Two, how you do it by pulling back in your chest and throat. Then you have Step Three undoing it which also allows you to unbond from your stance of not upsetting your client or she may get sick. You can experience your own fear of a structured bond or a more assertive bond where you would be assertive. Now you are harmonizing and supporting like a parent who encourages dependency or repressed aggression.

T: I now see that my own attitude discourages my client from forming more of an assertive stance. And my attitude is rooted in my own family history and emotional posture of trying to be a good person.

S.K: We could summarize this case with a diagram that shows the interaction between the client and the therapist:

ANN	THERAPIST
I want support without control. `--------------------------->`	
	I will support you but need to have control. `<--------------------------`
I want connection but pick men who are too demanding. `--------------------------->`	
	I connect with you at the mouth-breast level. `<--------------------------`
I want to be a part of, be cared for, be dependent. `--------------------------->`	
	I care for you, but don't make self-assertive demands. `<--------------------------`
I want to feel more self-assertive yet not be separated. `--------------------------->`	
	I can't give you that, I have to now control your contact. `<-------------------------->`
This is just like the past, I am defeated.	

Ann seeks a young woman's contact and is offered childlike contact. She wants connection and is offered distance. The struggle is over control, what bond will be formed—that which Ann seeks or that which the therapist offers.

Betty and Greg:
A Case Study of Seduction and Rejection

Greg: I would like to present a female client and use some pictures of her to understand the therapeutic situation. Betty is a divorced woman in her forties, with two grown children, who was previously married to a lawyer. She left him four years ago and has run through a succession of men since then, and, according to her, they are all the same kind of male, dependent then they turn against her. They become more demanding, asking to be taken care of. One is a recovering alcoholic, another is a successful businessman who appears to be powerful but isn't. She is a disappointed person. The issue for me is that I perceive her as a very angry person and I am reluctant to work with her anger.

Stanley Keleman: Why do you think she is angry?

Greg: She is like a hurt, angry child when she talks about one or other of these men or her former husband. It is like she has been deprived of something by life.

S.K: Like what?

Greg: She is not being taken care of.

S.K: Why are you afraid of her anger? Are you frightened of it in yourself?

Greg: I have been over the years. I recall not being able to deal with my mother's anger as a growing boy. It was very frightening to me. I also recall my aunt telling me not to be angry with her. So I am reluctant to confront anger head on in another woman who is about my mother's age when I was young. She is a strong woman. She is a social worker in a very innovative social agency and is reputed to be very good at what she does.

S.K: What does she come to you for?

Greg: She came with a sense of disarray and a loss of direction in her life. We have dealt with that successfully for about six months.

S.K: How did you deal with that?

Greg: By bringing to her attention how much she is governed by her beliefs about what she should do, what is the proper thing to do.

S.K: As you discuss this with me, I feel there is disorganization in your presentation. You are tentative, there is no discussion of what you have learned from Betty's structure. So I am trying to uncover what your working image is and what you are trying to do with her. This means to use Step One, to get an image of the situation and then to see how you and she use yourselves and each other.

It sounds as if you are making an unformed bond based on "take care of me" on Betty's side and "don't threaten me" on your side. I am not sure how angry this woman is. You talk about her picking weak men who then turn out to fit a pattern of disappointment. What would you make of the person that is shown in these pictures structurally, emotionally, and psychologically?

Greg: My first perception is of the square shoulders and the amount of energy in the chest, something going on up there. Secondly, my image is of the softness in the belly. My third image is of her legs, they appear not to be grounded but to be like sticks.

S.K: Do you like this woman?

Greg: Yes, I feel good about her.

S.K: How much do you like her?

Greg: Enough to keep on working with her.

S.K: Do you like her enough to keep on being confused by her and avoiding her anger and intensity?

Greg: That could be.

S.K: Let us start with that, your liking and your confusion.

Greg: I put myself in a position of liking somebody which automatically prevents me from perceiving something that is useful or speaking forthrightly to the person. I try to listen. I stop being inwardly responsive and start analyzing what is said, putting it into categories.

S.K: Betty looks like a mesomorphic overactive structure, an action person, a doer, with a weak lower body, a person who will set up situations of challenge and provocation, and want to do things, and get things done. Yet, her unsureness, lack of self-trust, and need for emotional support lies underneath all her testing. There is a clash between the mesomorphic part,—"I am strong, I want to be dominant"—and the diffuse, unorganized, lower half which seeks support,—"I can't, I don't want to be dominant." It appears that the dominant half compensates for the unformed half. I wonder whether you are being set up by Betty to be competent and unthreatening, being asked to be supportive and parental but not a male?

Greg: I have been sucked in and I am not clear about how to deal with it.

S.K: You set yourself up by your own need to be effective. You are challenged and taken in to give support.

Greg: I feel that. I ask myself how I have let this happen. I have a sense that I have an ideal of being effective rather than behaving as effective. I say to myself, "you are doing fine," but I miss what is really going on. I get stiff and attentive to give the impression of potency. But I really am seduced by the woman's vitality and calmness and miss the dependency.

S.K: Is she like your mother?

Greg: Yes, in the energy in her face, the strong eyes.

S.K: What do you do with that?

Greg: I back off. I draw in, try to move away. I use my body to convey an attitude, "I am in control," "I am strong," while I mask my fear with rigidity. Then I try to prove myself, prove that I am manly, in control by lifting my chest up. I assume a posture of bravado and bluff. From the outside it appears that I am stronger, but the inside feeling is unsure, pulling away.

S.K: Did the vitality of your mother both excite and frighten you? Proving you are effective means to control and hide yourself. This pulling away serves as protection and bonds you to your own and your mother's excitement. Why did Betty leave her husband?

Greg: She says he was too nice, quiet, peaceful. He never resisted her, she never got anything to push against.

S.K: That would fit her mesomorphic look. The contradictions in her pictures is the well-shaped vital, upper body and an unshaped pelvis. There is a discrepancy in the pulsation invested in the upper and outer body compared to the lower body. The upper and outer covers up or hides the submissive or unbounded lower part, tough cop versus soft cop, adult versus adolescent, "I am somebody," versus "I am nobody," "I can take care of myself," versus "I want to be cared for;" "I am aggressive" versus "I am submissive." This contradiction gives a clue why she would pick people who would have to disappoint her. One part or the other, the top or the bottom, will feel betrayed and let down. This is why she gets angry and feels disappointed in men. When her pulsatory assertiveness is not responded to, it leads to the disappointment of her upper part. The weak pulsation in the lower body creates disappointment for men and resentment for Betty. So you are talking about the postpersonal strength versus prepersonal-instinctual weakness. Her dominant upper statement is "I can do it," "I do do it," "I want you to match me." But her lower body says "no," "I can't," "help me," "Don't challenge me."

Greg: I don't want to disappoint her so I get sucked in to her "can you match me?" or her "can you help me?"

S.K: You are excited and challenged and then asked to be her support, her legs. So there is confusion about performance between controlling your responses and being manly and acting as her support. Show me physically how you use yourself to organize confusion.

Greg: When she projects dominance and then submission, she controls me. She elicits my support by my need to prove myself and please her. I work to give her support. I hold my own emotional assertiveness back.

S.K: How?

Greg: By pulling back and stiffening my spine, clenching my jaw, raising my chest, and tensing my shoulders and pelvis.

S.K: Do it more. What emotional stance is this?

Greg: It feels on the surface like pride, but deeper down it feels like I am bracing to be hit or I am scared. When I release the upper bracing, I feel excited.

S.K: Is that how you make yourself ineffective emotionally?

Greg: She keeps coming back so she must gain something from that. I suppose the challenge to prove ourselves is what keeps our bond going.

S.K: There is a confused connection between you. The dual situation she finds herself in is represented in you. The vital assertions of her upper body affect you and yet you avoid the feelings of dependency in the lower half. Do you avoid the anger of this woman? Is your statement, "I don't want to get this woman angry," or "I must not let her gain control," or does it mean "I fear the excitement, I dare not satisfy her?" Let us repeat the exercise of how you control yourself.

Greg: I pull back and up. I brace myself. I don't want to feel my own pulsation in my chest or pelvis. I say I have to be strong, prove I can control myself. In that way I do not feel her weakness, only the excitement I get from her challenge.

S.K: How do you use this?

Greg: When I deprogram it, I experience an excitement in me and an anger. I say to myself, "stop, stop, stop." "I don't want to be your son or your father."

S.K: You could use this woman's strength as the starting point. You could ask her to learn her pattern of demand and challenge and how it gives her a feeling of strength. Gradually, she will get to feel her weakness and sense of confusion. As you soften you will diminish your own fear of receiving strong pulsations in the upper face, chest. You could challenge your way of not taking care of, and the wanting-to-prove yourself pattern. At the same time you could demand that she deprogram the challenge and begin to take care of herself.

I would ask how she organizes herself to avoid her dependency and gets others to form a dependency bond with her. I would explore how she uses herself to be helpless and to "parent," how she bonds in an adult way and in a mouth-breast way. I would explore how you use yourself as her implied savior. So there are two bonds: one, overactive, dominating, controlling, and adult-like; the other, childlike, demanding, passive, and incorporating. This dual somatic-emotional structure accounts for the mixed messages and the mixed bond of control and connection and the terror of being separate and separated. Betty's strong mouth-breast connection may be a clue to how deeply rooted the fear of lack of identity is about her womanness. Your need to control yourself, back away from the excitement of her upper body also attracts the sucked-into, "take care of me" of her lower body. Your rigidity invites her unformed attachment as well as her challenges. She may choose disappointing men in order to feel safe because of the dependency in her lower body. "I project strength, I hide weakness. If I control you I feel disappointed. If you contact me in the lower half of my body, and make demands on me, I feel disappointed." Greg, you set yourself up to hold back as a way to be bonded to her.

Greg: When I work with my upper body, increasing the awareness of my pulling back or holding back in my arms and shoulders, there comes a spontaneous softening and a reaching out. Sadness and longing come up. When I work with her lower structure to increase form and a sense of backbone by asking her to do what I do with my upper body, pull in, be firm, there develops in her "Don't come close sexually, don't take advantage of my unformedness."

S.K: You may, as a man, supply a sense of emotional presence and identity which gives her a sense of contact and a feeling of her inside. Your bonding "I come to you," or "I stick with you," changes to "I can let you come to me. I do not have to invalidate you." She can then begin to experience her inner feeling and learn to bond from it. Rather than control and connection, you have contact and self-management. This gives satisfaction which is contact over time. Contact involves meeting and maintaining this connection over time. This gives a personal sense of self and others that has to be worked for. It is working to maintain those individual personal connections through a range of different experiences that forms one's mature pulsatory bonds with another. Maintaining contact with self and others is where satisfaction is. That is central to working somatically with another or with one's self. The ability to form a life, to maintain long term contacts has to do with a person's emotional way of bonding. In concrete language that means when you do somatic work you teach a person a personal way to form pulsation into personal expression, a personal bond.

In this situation, Greg appears to be strong by his rigidity and his statement "here I am." He uses himself to project strength and control. She comes disorganized, helpless, creating confusion, being helpless, showing competence and controlling. She has contact with Greg as a child, a mouth-breast connection of "respond to my demands," and as a dominating mother. But she means, "take care of me, don't act like I am an adult sexual person." This is a mixed bond where the client wishes the therapist to be both equal and unequal. "Like me, accept me, let me dominate," says Betty. "I can perform and control your needs, don't be angry with me, don't be out of control," says Greg. This bond forms a collusion as neither person is being adult. Each seeks to control the other thereby creating a clouded connection. The performing attitude of both the therapist and client is found in their upper body—chest, head, neck, arms. This posture seeks to keep away, push away, cling and hold onto while inviting dependency. Greg says, "Depend on me," and, also, "I expect you to excite me." Betty says, "Let me depend on you but I must be in control." Greg says, "I won't go away nor threaten you but will act parental or like a son." She says, "Don't take advantage of me, let me depend on you to take care of me, be my father or be my brother or son." Both of you need to dismantle the pseudo-adult, controlling, performing posture of the upper body. This will show that her bond has been to confuse the other and make him disappointing. The real bond is not to be an adult but to be in control which is equated with adulthood. The confusion for both of you is the clash between the loss of control and the inability to give up control.

How do you feel about her demand to dominate, to be taken care of?

Greg: It makes me angry and resentful.

S.K: How do you express that?

Greg: I move away.

S.K: From her or from your own anger? You need to recognize your own anger rather than control hers. So you lift your chest, stiffen your spine, pull back and perform like a good boy for mother. This may confuse Betty who feels your performance as control and strength. Your posture says "stay away from me" even though it looks like cooperation.

Greg: I see that I really try to please my mother by doing what is proper and performing well to avoid her anger as well as my own. And in this way I also say, "I reject you while I try to please you."

S.K: What needs to be done is to disorganize the pleasing, performing pattern and bond and let the excited pulsation form a new bond. The confusion in this bonding has to do with not being able to make the transition from mouth-breast, from control to contact. The confusion is structured in you as "taking care of" and "I don't want to control myself and perform." In Betty it is "Let me dominate and control, yet take care of me." In this way the need for connection is maintained as you try to resolve the confusion. You, Greg, make a bond where you let this woman use you, that is, you try to please her as your way to be connected. She tries to control you to protect herself from becoming a genital victim. In challenging your structure of confusion—how you pull back, turn away, stay there but hold back, disassociated from your wish not to perform—you will discover your anger and how you are supposed to please and not be a threat to the woman. You then face the situation of not performing, and letting the female separate.

I would imagine that when Betty begins to challenge and destructure Step Two, her dominating and competing stance, you will see thrashing about, diffusion, a lack of focus, and a searching attitude in her pelvis. This is the need to control others and her fear of submission, a pattern of "Don't use me." Hopefully, she will begin to see that she wants support and contact for an emerging adult form which will permit individuality and separateness. The experience of her own pulsatory pelvic feelings can be then used to help her learn to incorporate these into assertion and containment, and to learn that she gives form to her feelings and creates a bond where people both make demands and care for each other. In this way sexual contact does not become a dependency connection but two separate people coming together.

Bob and Cy:
A Case Study of Male Bonding

Bob: My client, Cy, is always prepared for rejection. Cy is thirty-nine, he has an older brother and a younger sister. He was married once while he was a student. When he came out of the university, he taught for several years but now works with disabled children. He divorced his wife because he resented taking care of her, could not get along with her, and did not understand her demands. After the divorce he went off to live in a commune in the mountains, went through two drug-induced psychotic breakdowns, and after his first breakdown he became a follower of an Indian guru. He has been with this group for eight years. He has a split in himself about committing to a spiritual path. He rejects it even though he tells himself he should not. His presenting complaint was the split between his emotional self and his rational self, a split he sees as being strong versus being weak, being free versus being needy. Until the age of eighteen he was punished by his father, spanked, sent to his room, deprived of dinner. He deals with his down periods when he is depressed by something he calls clumping, getting into bed and curling up into a ball and staying there until he feels like emerging. Recently, he met a woman who works with children as a social worker. He is scared because she might make too many demands on him, demand to be taken care of, stay at home, maybe even adopt a child.

If you look at his pictures you see a very compressed stomach, like the California muscleman ideal, pushing up his chest, and tension in his neck and shoulders. Whenever I get close to something emotional, I notice his face, jaw, neck, and how it tightens up as if to hold on. A lot of his function is to hold on. He has had two destructuring psychotic episodes, so I have to be cautious. In my work with him, I try to get him to let down into himself so he can be aware of how he holds himself. My long range question is how to deal with the rejection, how he organizes it, how he tries to ward off assertion and ambition. My concern is having him collapse on me.

Stanley Keleman: The general characteristic of Cy is rigidity and stiffness. He pulls away from his genitals and the ground and pulls back from people. He is so stiff he becomes unbounded, so spastic he can't be in himself. Cy wasn't getting enough attention, his wife didn't take care of him, yet he needed her to work to earn money. He retreated to a commune to get away from the world. He destructured his adult accomplishments with drugs and retreated from his societal and personal self as a way to enter the prepersonal realm where his unconscious ran wild and innundated him with desires and images. Cy is either in a depressive or regressive mouth-breast or umbilical state. He hungers for a supportive structure but he seeks it through others rather than through himself. The split between his emotions and his rational self is really a conflict between the impulses of a child, a prepersonal umbilical world, and his hunger for male form and structure. He is an adultified child, an educated adult and an emotional kid, seeking an early bond on the mouth-breast level. He seeks connection and attention and demands to be the special child, to be embedded in the other, to be reconnected. Cy's split is between present reality and past fantasy, between the socially realistic and the instinctual given, between his inner child and his outer adult, between uncontained and contained pulsation. Cy bonds prepersonally; he avoids adult bonds or undermines them.

How Cy organizes himself to get support, to feel important, to be one of the children is what is important. He forms bonds with children or with other unbounded people as a child. Through destructuring, he seeks to be released from his pulsations and hungers for containment and engulfs himself with others in a global sea of undifferentiation. He forms childlike or infant bonds.

Bob: I think he plays man, acting grown-up.

S.K: Cy looks and sounds formless. He says he wants to resolve his split, be spiritual and rational rather than emotional. What I think he means is to live in the world of men or women in an undifferentiated way. I feel it is an error not to challenge your own empathy. In dealing with Cy, his story blinds you. You overempathize with his story rather than looking at how he tells it and how he tries to deform a connection and create a bond from a formless state.

Bob: Are you suggesting that I am only listening to his story, not his structure?

S.K: Somehow you don't resonate with how he uses himself. You are caught in a collusion of empathy, joining with his image of himself as a victim. You do not see his rebellion or his not refusal to work. Your enemy, Bob, is your good will.

Bob: You mean my need for good will.

S.K: Your need to make an ally of the client.(Step One)

Bob: That fits. I do that a lot.

S.K: How is it organized? (Step Two) How do you use yourself to express concern?

Bob: It seems to me that I approach it the opposite way, I harden myself by raising and squeezing my chest and compressing myself.

S.K: Organize it more, make the squeezing more intense until you feel it. Now disorganize it slightly.(Step Three) Now disorganize it more, then more, then more. Give up compressing to invoke concern.

Bob: I feel something loosening in my chest, and then a rising warm feeling. It feels like a need to cry or reach out. The words are, "Nobody listened to me, nobody took my cry seriously." That fits perfectly. The story of my life is trying to be taken seriously. I have never been able to put this in words before.

S.K: Step Four gives you insight. It tells you that your need to be taken seriously or listened to emotionally becomes your bond of collusion. That is the contract you enter into with a client, "I will listen to you and take you seriously, then you will listen to me." What we have then is a bond of collusive cooperation, to receive and be received, an adult form of a mouth-breast feeling. To do this you suspend your adult reality perception and organize a rigid attitude of listening.

Cy bonds by destructuring, eruption, incorporating you in global pulsations, by sobbing, complaining, getting you to listen, projecting onto you "the empathetic parent." He penetrates you like a child pesters his parents, he then sucks you into him. You project "I will take you seriously" which is your need to be taken seriously. In this you feel your own longing. How do you try to suppress this cry in you? (Step Two)

Bob: I compress my diaphragm and throat. I purse my lips, suck them in. I have a feeling, "Come here, I need you."

S.K: Just like Cy does.

Bob: Oh my God, you are right. I am amazed. My image is that I keep myself bottled up in here in my throat and chest like in a cage.

S.K: When you loosen it, (Step Three) what happens? (Step Four)

Bob: When I experience something rising there, I rush out and do something. When I now tighten this, pull in, suck in my face and release it, I feel I want to cry "Take me seriously, I want to connect with you." "To get this connection I will be interested in what you tell me."

S.K: Being concerned is the way you feel connected and in contact with him. It is how you and he create a parent-child bond. You are his "good parent," he is you as a child. Your rigidity and his rigidity empathize, harmonize, resonate. You have a bonding of like structures and need. However, you, Bob, have an adult form with a child inside whereas Cy has a frozen child form which wishes to be connected to another, never separated. That threatens you because you wish to be taken seriously. You don't want to be a parent to a child that won't grow up. You wanted your own father to listen to you, to share with you, and to help you separate from your mother.

Don't you think Cy is blackmailing you by saying "I'll bomb out, take acid, go crazy and be irresponsible if you don't care for me" or "I'll never surrender my need to be bonded to my mother?"

Bob: Yes! I also wanted to love my father, to bond with him. He was so damn perfect he forced me back upon my mother.

S.K: I think Cy wishes to bond umbilically, rest in you and grow like a fetus. He wants to belong, not to give or share. You wish to be connected by sharing your male self and being in your father's world.

Bob: I fear that unstructured place. I pull in when I recall how my mother always wanted me to care for her. That makes me quite angry but now I feel that anger because my father did not allow me to be close.

S.K: How can you separate from your father's demand not to be close, your response of pulling back, and your statement "I tried to listen to him, it didn't work, he rejected me?"

Bob: When I undo my rigidity and pulling back, I feel an urge to push away. The accompanying statement is "get out of here." But I never follow through on this statement because it scares me not to have had an accepting father. But I guess at one level I am rejecting Cy's demand just like my father rejected mine. At another level I am trying to be taken seriously.

S.K: You could stop asking him to take you seriously. You think Cy wishes to work for a living, but he doesn't. You need to show him how he is constantly destructuring bonds or never allowing them to form. How will you dismantle your need to be taken seriously? Maybe when you reorganize your attitude of concern and accept your own inner pulsation you will not be seduced by the pulsations that remind you of your mother and the fear of your father. Then you may be more realistic about his demands and help him see that his own cry is really for form. Perhaps if you push his story away and reject his destructuring attitude it will push him into himself and begin to establish self-containment and cooperative bonds. To do this requires more than sharing thoughts and insights; it requires actions, gestures, and postures that organize this behavior.

This situation looks like an adult mouth-breast bond described as emotion versus rationality or as Cy's urge towards individuality versus his communal life. Bob fears Cy's tendency to unbound his personal and social structure. He doesn't see its destructive component. Cy wants to undo his adult form and be carried around, implanted, taken inside the other. Bob's fear is his reaction to his own crying, he wants to prevent it. Cy wants to bond in Step Four, incubation. He wants to live in an undifferentiated state. It is just like an embryo. Bob's attitude is to get him to accept organization, Step Two, structure and realism. Bob has to insist that Cy work on his problem and form an adult which is different than the injunction to be one, to let Cy be a boy with his father, a boy who wants to form an adult.

What Bob has to undo in himself is his wish for a father who will listen to him. By taking down his own rigidity, the boy seeking to be heard, he can form a bond where he can become a father and let Cy's boy grow.

Bob: So I try to get him to be an adult without seeing he is incapable of doing so unless he changes his form of contact with me. He has a connection but he has to learn to deal with separations, demands, and rejection and he must support these values by action.

S.K: Yes. Cy may wish to form a boy into a man, to bond with you eventually as an adult male. He fears this and is angry and destructive. I see Cy as being in Step Four not Step Three. He swings between destroying adult form, Step Three, where there is minimum structure and the return to the mother world or womb of Step Four, the pleasure of uninhibited pulsation supplied without effort. Cy avoids male form, male values, male cooperation.

Bob: Yes, I believe Cy has little structure and this frightens and scares me. I need structure, my tight throat, my need to listen. I love Cy's rationality and form a collusion with it. I relate order and structure with rationality but our bonding is not based on that but on taking each other seriously.

S.K: But your need for order forms a male bond. To disorganize your own structure frightens you. However, you have to let Cy organize form even if it makes him anxious and depressed. Maybe he can form a cooperative work bond with you if you reject his victim stance and your own need to be listened to.

This case teaches something about the male to male bond, how a client bonds to a therapist as a "good mommy" but is really looking for a "good daddy." The rigidity of both therapist and client serves to avoid their pain around their rejecting fathers. Bob's rigidity says, "I can take it, I can control my crying." Cy's stiffness says, "I refuse to let men or women enter me." Cy's rigidity converts longing into rebellion, anger, and destructuring. His spastic rigidity serves to avoid male companionship or male bonding. Bob is not as rigid as Cy, he can accept another, he can be receptive whereas Cy is terrified of receptivity. Bob forms the bond by being big and identifying with the boy in Cy. Cy becomes small and turns the male therapist into a female, someone who is receptive and accepting. If Bob can destructure his fear about losing control, he can then bond with Cy in a male way, help him accept his own maleness, and teach him about the male world of cooperation.

This case further illustrates that bonding involves a connection to members of one's own gender as well as to the opposite, for without this, one makes lop-sided choices, fuses instead of connects, makes separation rather than distance. The swing between the two poles of similars and opposites is the essence of individuality.

This case also teaches something about psychotherapy. Is psychotherapy interested in solving a riddle or only diagnosis and remedial action? Somatic therapy is mystery, investigation, seeing how things are organized. A therapist helps form bonds for the client to learn about his own somatic-emotional patterns. The heart of somatic therapy is the organization of how a client presents himself as well as the therapist's response. The knowledge of the bonding process, the concrete experience of your own and the client's muscular emotional expression, leads to the therapeutic insight as to how the client bonds to you and how he permits you to bond to him and how, together, you can form a variety of new bonds.

Lecture Five

As presented in these lectures, transference has multiple dimensions:

- Transference is bonding—how a client and therapist establish a relationship based on the degrees of closeness and distance that each desires.

- Transference involves a developmental sequence:
    - umbilical
    - mouth-breast
    - genital
    - body-to-body

- Transference can further be understood as which layer of the self—prepersonal, personal, postpersonal—seeks contact, connection, or control.

- Transference involves distortions of the pulsatory continuum—how structures that are rigid, dense, swollen, and collapsed seek to relate to a therapist.

- The Five Steps are the means to disorganize and reorganize the bonding relationship.

Transference and countertransference refer to emotional bonds that are distorted by the client's need to have the therapist be what he wants or vice versa, for example, a client wants his therapist to be cooperative or resistant. In order for bonding or emotional connection to happen, it is necessary that a whole symphony of somatic-emotional events take place. For example, a client speaks in a particular way, postures himself so that his heart begins to beat faster, or his brain begins to associate the therapist with memories and images of past events. The client is flushed with old and new feelings and seeks responses from his therapist to suit his need to be helpless, or angry, or loving. Bonding thus involves a somatic organization of the self which may or may not be conscious to the client or the therapist.

As a therapist, you respond to your client's emotional-muscular signals with your own organization. You cringe, become passive, brace for attack, soften in seductive behavior, rise above it with indifference, or are seduced into caring because his signals for help mobilizes your need to be a parent or an authority.

Somatic postures play as important a part as words, explanations, and interpretations do. For it is through these somatic-emotional organizations that the client learns acceptance and new ways of organizing behavior. Acceptance is more than words or actions, it is the state of the therapist receiving the client. Too many times authorities tell us they like us or act as our friends, yet, we experience rejection. When others speak and act differently than our experience of them, we become confused.

The communication of somatic-emotional states between therapist and client is an organized dyad seeking either to perpetuate itself or organize another form. The mature nervous system of the adult is the teacher for the infant. But the adult organizes more than parental behavior for a child. What is organized is an individual relationship that keeps forming and growing all of one's life. In this same way, therapeutic bonding is meant to organize a relationship that is capable of many levels of experience, from the prepersonal experience of oneness to the separate, individualistic connection of gendered communion.

Somatic-emotional attitudes of the client and responses by the therapist are what is central to bonding. They are what organizes transference and countertransference. Indifference, distance, objectivity forms one kind of relationship. Responsiveness to the client's behavior forms another. If we act out our responses on the client, another, more dangerous, response forms.

This understanding is even more significant when a therapist uses somatic-emotional methods—touching, doing specific body exercises, or engaging clients in somatic-imaginative exercises. In evoking basic somatic states while remaining aloof or unresponsive, a therapist creates the same state that existed in the client's childhood, aroused children and unresponsive parents or aroused children and over-responsive parents. Responsiveness organizes a state for the client which gives birth to his particular way of doing things, how he organizes a form that makes him an individual while relating to others.

The main point in all transference is that the client wishes to organize and form a relationship in accordance with his own principles of differentiation. We each seek to do things our own way. Paradoxically, we also yearn to be cooperative, to be part of a family, to belong. Many forms of therapy help a client by giving him a sense of belonging, but these approaches may compromise the client's own way of doing things. Other therapies suggest that client autonomy is won by giving up connection to others. Yet separateness is different than separation, individuality different than individualism. Each person has a need for separateness. We want to relate in a differentiated way, neither severed nor fused.

Therapeutic bonding is a continually shifting process with many stages of initiation and testing for both the therapist and client. Each stage of the process of re-establishing emotional growth begins to organize the next stage until a form of relationship is established in which the depth of the contact and communication allows for separation as well as satisfaction. More importantly, this relationship establishes an intimacy for the client with his own process of somatic-emotional organization which the client can then apply to other aspects of his life. Transference and countertransference not only heal by reorganizing past hurts and inadequacies of contact, but they establish a process of individuation and personal freedom that can form a client's life.

Bonding involves complex organization. In order to create a bond, a client must structure his behavior. Pulsation, feeling, excitation, and sensation must be organized and projected along with an expectation from the past. The response the client receives is then introjected or rejected. Bonding, therefore, involves not only feelings and images, but, more importantly, somatic-muscular patterns. The full organization of this is what has to be understood.

I recall a client telling me about his mother (Step One) while at the same time compressing his arms to his side as if to control himself (Step Two). It was this compression which constituted the link between being cared for and humiliation. It was my sense of this somatic-muscular constriction that alerted me to his emotional dilemma regarding love and shame, an unknown pattern he was living out. The actions that he engaged in (Step Two), exaggerated and intensified, for example, "Look how you compress yourself, do it over and over again," helped this client know both his action and its history. In this way he learned both what he did (Steps Three and Four) and a means to undo it.

The ability to disorganize what has been organized is the key to solving the transference. When the pattern is disorganized, old introjections, other people's identity that we structure as ourself, dissolve. At the end of the disorganization is a place where emotional response is free of the personal past, the search for love, the vitality of desire. A client enters an unconditioned state in which he finds new ways to know his past and be in the present.

If a client fails to disorganize part of his hurtful behavior, he tends not to reform or reorganize his patterns but repeats them until they are exhausted. Repetition occurs because a client out of fear or ignorance does not disorganize. He may not have outer-world contact which allows him to practice new behavior, thus, he stays on the old paths and repeats his pain.

Bonding as a System

Somatic-emotional therapy is a system of interaction between a stable pole, the therapist and an unstable pole, the client, an organized pole and an unorganized pole. It is the function of the more stable and organized pole to assist the less stable pole. The therapist is an organizer for the client as an immature organism needs an adult structure to help organize itself into adulthood.

Transference activates a bonding system, a series of interacting relationships involving different roles and shapes. The uterine bond is based upon fusion, the therapist and the client become one. The therapist's role is to be the womb, the incubator while the client takes the role of the embryo, the structure that is given to without limits. The mouth-breast bond is based on hunger and demand. The therapist and client are separate yet their relationship is exclusive like a mother and her infant. The therapist's role is to be the needed other, a source of nourishment while the client takes the role of hunger and need. In genital-to-genital bonding the therapist and client establish an intimate and close connection. The therapist accepts and socializes the client's genital projections and helps transfer them to the outer world. To this end the therapist accepts the role of love object, fantasied intimate, or brother or sister. With body-to-body bonding the relationship becomes one of family member, friend, and equal. The therapist acts as older brother, father, big sister, aunt, or teacher. For the client, the therapist is inside and outside, intimate and distant, stable and changing, someone they lock onto yet separate from. The therapist represents all these layers of bonding.

The goal of this system is both growth and individuation. All embryos, fetuses, and small children seek their next level of develop-ment. They are pushed to it internally even as they are pulled toward it by the older, more grown-up parents and society. The parent is the pole that attracts the child towards growth just as the child deepens the adult by evoking the parent's past. The parent, then, relives his own experience or corrects the pains and errors he encountered in growing up. Likewise in therapy, a therapist acts as the pole that attracts the client towards individuation, provided the therapist recognizes and accepts different bonding situations as part of the growth process.

As the client projects onto the therapist and evokes responses, a resonating process is established. This is a process of pulsation in which waves of somatic emotional expansion and contraction, projection and introjection organize fields of cellular activity into patterns of complex behavior. Self-intimacy increases as does intimacy with another. The deep feelings that give life meaning rise to the surface seeking expression or containment.

The transference and countertransference situation organizes experience into a form that represents those experiences on the cellular, emotional, psychological, and somatic levels. A client re-experiences with his therapist the forming of his personal body, feelings, memories, and adventures. Therapy reconstitutes an inhibited or hibernated developmental process. A client and therapist meet and set up a pattern of interaction, head to head, language to language, belly to belly, heart to heart. Pulsations of need and expectation, desire and response are exchanged. The therapist receives the projections of the client, bonds appropriately, and organizes the insights, feelings, thoughts, and somatic postures which the client introjects to form his own identity.

Action Patterns: The Key Ingredient

Bonding is evoked not only by talking about the client's needs and disappointments, analyzing his dreams and fantasies, resurrecting his early feelings or role within the family of origin but, primarily, through the somatic postures and expressions the client and therapist take or are unable to take. For example, reaching out, standing up for one's self, pushing another away, the involuntary movements of crying or sucking. These postures seek connection and response from the therapist.

In somatic emotional work, patterns of organismic response precede feelings and intuitions. In *Your Body Speaks Its Mind* (Center Press, 1975) I discuss the role of attitudes and the formative process and show that the latent state of the organism is already an action pattern, a series of innate, neural, emotional, muscular patterns, to grasp, to suck, to reach out, to attack, to withdraw, that is invoked whenever a situation calls for it.

In somatic work, transference refers specifically to the muscular, emotional, attitudinal postures on the part of both the client and therapist, as they establish a connection that reflects a past pain or unknown parts of themselves. Transference is the action of the client to reach out in a specific way. Likewise the therapist's readiness to respond to the client is an action pattern whether the therapist is aware of it or not. For example, a therapist believes he responds with empathy, or observation, or intuition when, in fact, his first response is the neural muscular pattern either to receive or ward off. About a particular client he says, "when I am with I get a stiff neck," or "I have certain associations," or "I get anxious" and analyzes this as "resistance" to the client. In fact, he may be resisting his own somatic patterns or responses, his reactions to the unknown, or to being aroused. More importantly, the therapist's resistance may be his inability to respond or suspend a response to get close or retreat. Unknowingly he stiffens his legs, arms, and hands, invoking patterns of getting ready to run and the feeling, "I've got to get away."

In somatic work the somtic and emotional response of the therapist is what is central. Somatic process focuses on the organismic response of bonding with its accompanying thoughts, feelings, and images. To the degree that a therapist is not aware of his neural, emotional, muscular responses, he tends to project them as what is going on in the client. He accuses the client of holding on, of being invasive or resistant. At the same time he is probably unaware of his own attempts to invade his client. A therapist may hold his breath, suspend his action, and soften the muscles of his abdomen in order to be receptive. A dependent client adopts a stance of looking up and assumes a posture that makes him smaller. A therapist may wish to be an accepting authority yet his somatic emotional posture is stiff-spined, tight-lipped, standoffish and sends the message, "I don't accept you, I am not receptive to you. keep your distance." Further-more, he may have little awareness that this is his stance.

So the need to bond or to restructure obsolete bonds is what somatic therapy is all about. And the somatic-emotional attitudinal postures are the real message that is going back and forth. The client wants to bond in a way that he is only dimly aware of, while the therapist responds, hopefully, with his own somatic awareness of what the client is saying and how he instinctively responds. A client may wish to bond body-to-body but the therapist is so identified with his role as helper that he cannot unstructure it and be the one who accompanies the client, or allow himself to be the listener while the client tries out patterns of domination.

Somatic Mirroring

A client's body attitude and state mirrors his inner feeling and experience. The client presents himself on ever deeper layers, here I am as withholder, plodder, etc. He hopes the therapist sees him and reflects back who he is. The therapist does so by his own somatic processes that mirror his internal responses. He tightens his jaw or holds his breath. Hopefully, the therapist is aware of how he responds muscularly and emotionally and knows what he projects and what his responses are to his client's projections. The therapist conveys to the client his receptivity or distance by his somatic-emotional posture.

Mirroring somatic-emotional postures is a projection-introjection process. The client transfers or projects himself onto the therapist in order to know himself. "I need a father, I assume the posture of a son in relation to a male authority. I become compliant, obedient, rebellious, defiant. Once again, I sense the father-son bond." The therapist's response mirrors back either the authoritarian father, a rigid posture, or the accepting father, a softer posture. The client can then bond differently with other men.

This mirroring process is somatic. It is not by words or emotions that a state is conveyed but by the raised or softened chest, the stiff or soft belly, the tense or relaxed jaw and eyes. The practicality of the mirror image is that it enables the therapist to sense the bond sought by the client by what posture the client adopts. The therapist can then direct the attention of the client to his somatic posture and what it may be signifying and assist the client in learning his own internal language. Finally, the mirror image enables the therapist to discover his own responses and what kind of bond he seeks.

Somatic-emotional therapy deals with an organized, somatic, generalized state—rigid, dense, swollen, collapsed—that expresses itself in the multiple images it creates. The state is first an internalized experience which then becomes an externalized expression seeking a bond and a response from the other. For example, in uterine bonding a client senses a missing piece in his internal organization and externalizes this in a motor attitude, seeking from the therapist a womb to encompass him. The client's action attempts to evoke a specific response from the therapist. The response he receives is read back by the client in light of the bond he knowingly or unknowingly attempts to form. The therapist, unaware of his somatic response, believes that his image of himself is what the client is responding to. Yet it is the underlying somatic emotional postures and expressions on the part of both the client and the therapist that is the basic dialogue. It is this aspect of somatic therapy that differentiates it from more traditional therapy where transference is viewed as feelings, emotions, fantasies, and images. Somatic therapy analyzes bodily gestures and attitudinal expressions as the real mirrors of feeling and need. Somatic therapy sees the interaction of somatic-emotional postures and gestures on the part of the therapist and client as that which establishes the bond or on-going system between them. Further, it is the awareness of and the ability to disorganize and reorganize these somatic expressions that is the main work in somatic therapy.

The Bond of Loving and Being Loved

Transference is an emotional process that seeks to form connection to another. It is rooted in deep and powerful waves of need accompanied by feelings of urgency and gratification. The urge to project onto another our hopes for satisfaction and love represents the continuation of our existence, growth, and individuation. Without this urge an individual would either die, be unfulfilled, stunted, or less than fully human.

Therefore, the order and logic of transference can only be understood emotionally. Transference involves the wish for love. Transference is the projection of emotional needs, to belong to, to be wanted, to be taken care of, to be protected, to be received, to be cared for, to be given to, to be intimate with. The client's projections are his pseudopod of bonding, they demand a response. The kind of response his projection receives determines the fate of his need.

Negative transference, likewise, involves a wish for emotional connection. Negative transference is a distorted bonding in which a client asserts his independence, masks his dependency, or distances the therapist by confusing him with somebody from the past. In negative transference a client tries to establish a bond of love through a mask that denies it.

Countertransference, in its largest sense, is the response to a client's projections. The therapist's somatic-emotional response forms the other side of the client's need to be cared for. Therefore it is dangerous for a therapist to act out his own unconscious or unlived part.

Transference is an effort by the client to open his heart and risk loving again. Transference carries with it the hope of being intimate. It means to venture out, to put onto another what cannot be accepted by one's self, and to finally take back and return to one's self what has been projected. Just as we long to belong, to be taken care of, to be given to, so do we learn, through transference, to let ourselves be taken in. Just as we want to be received, we learn to give, to internalize the other. Just as we yearn to be separate, we allow others to be separate. Just as we learn to embody our experience, we learn to embody the other.

The stages of transference and bonding are linked to our emotional development. The state of loving, belonging to, being part of, can be linked with the umbilical bond. To want, to demand, to be reunited is a part of the mouth-breast stage. To desire, to take, to be taken, to be together, then apart, then reconciled with the other are the qualities associated with the genital phase. To be intimate with one's self and with another, to love is the hallmark of the body to body phase. What is projected is the self, what is responded to is the self of the other, the self extends itself and creates a state with another in order to reveal itself to itself.

If the client's or therapist's emotional muscular patterns are fixated, they remain stuck in particular patterns, for example, spasticity in the organs of digestion, an underdeveloped brain or the muscles of sucking, the patterns of clinging or aggressively grabbing, pushing, pulling. All these patterns may be compulsively lived out in muscular stances of domination, attacking, or submission.

The continuum of bonding starts with being given to and ends as giving. This continuum goes from taking to giving, from projecting one's self to receiving the projections of another in an endless continuum of give and take, love and loving that serves the growth of the other and one's self. Transference starts with the need to be loved by having one's needs met and evolves to projecting the need to love. While it has been said that the love of the therapist cures, it is equally true that the love of the client, projected onto the therapist, and introjected back into himself, is a means whereby the client cures himself, and, maybe even the therapist.

Postscript

Somatic bonding teaches:

Receptivity
> how to be emotionally connected to another, yet remain in contact with one's self.

How to connect to another
> who is similar or opposite.

How to dismantle emotional connections
> and separate from another.

How to create emotional bonds that are
> flexible and personalized.

Most of all, bonding teaches
> that some bonds are involuntary, determined, destined, unpredictable.

Others are voluntary, chosen,
> capable of being influenced.

Some bonds are created
> and maintained, while others are not, and each of us has to learn how to live with this truth.

Center For Energetic Studies

The Center for Energetic Studies in Berkeley, California, under the direction of Stanley Keleman seeks to structure a modern contemplative approach to self-knowing and living in which one's own subjective process gives birth to a set of values which then guides the whole of one's life. Today's values are increasingly divorced from our deepest processes, and bodily experience has been misunderstood and relegated to second place.

Somatic reality is an emotional reality that is much larger than innate genetic patterns of behavior. Emotional reality and biological reality are the same and cannot be separated or distinguished. Biological ground also means gender, the male and female responses that are innate to human life, the sexual identity with which we are born. Somatic reality is at the very core of existence, the source of our deepest religious feelings and psychological perceptions.

Classes and programs at the Center offer a psycho-physical practicum that brings to the forefront the basic ways a person learns. The key issue is how we use ourselves—learning the language of how viscera and brain use muscle to create behavior. These classes teach the essential somatic aspect of all roles and dramatize the possibilities of action to deepen the sense of connection to the many worlds in which all of us participate.

For further information, write to:
Center for Energetic Studies
2045 Francisco Street
Berkeley, California 94709

ALSO BY STANLEY KELEMAN

Embodying Experience(1987)

Emotional Anatomy(1985)

In Defense of Hereosexuality(1982)

Somatic Reality(1979)

Your Body Speaks Its Mind(1975)

Living Your Dying(1974)

Human Ground:

Sexuality, Self and Survival(1971)

Todtmoos: A Book of Poems (1971)